CONTENTS

Quotations from AN INSPECTOR CALLS AND OTHER PLAYS by J. B. Priestley (these plays first published by William Heinemann 1948-50, first published by Penguin Books 1969, Penguin Classics 2000). 'An Inspector Calls' copyright 1947 by J. B. Priestley and Penguin Books Ltd.

INTRODUCTION

This guide was written by Andrew Bruff who, in 2011, had a vision to share his GCSE expertise in English language and literature. This resulted in his first online tutorial video at youtube.com/mrbruff.

Six years later, his videos have been viewed over 20 million times across 214 different nations. To accompany these videos, he has published over 20 revision guides, many of which are best sellers. His guides to the previous GCSEs in English language and literature topped the list of Amazon best sellers for over 45 weeks and achieved huge acclaim.

This guide to the AQA GCSE English literature exams aims to build on those strengths. It contains detailed help on every question in the exams. Please note that this book is not endorsed by or affiliated to any exam boards; Mr Bruff is simply an experienced teacher using his expertise to help students.

FREE GIFT: the ebook edition of this book contains colour images and links to exclusive free videos. You deserve those too, so email info@mrbruff.com with proof of purchase, and he will email you the ebook edition for free.

Follow Mr Bruff on Twitter @MrBruffEnglish or visit his website www.mrbruff.com for details of his range of GCSE and A level revision guides.

DEDICATION

Mr Bruff would like to thank a number of people who have been instrumental in supporting his work:

- Sunny Ratilal and Sam Perkins, who worked on the front cover design.
- Noah and Elijah, who lost their 'daddy' to the office far too many times in the completion of this book.
- Claire, his lovely wife, who got behind him in my vision and supports him in it every day.
- Chris Bruff—a brother who has put his money where his mouth is and supported the work that benefits so many.

Hello

Thank you so much for purchasing this revision guide. Everything that is covered in here is also covered in a corresponding set of videos which I have made neat and accessible on our terrific partner platform: **TuitionKit.**

On TuitionKit you'll be able to schedule all my revision videos from this booklet and others to help your organise your revision better, by breaking it down into easy to handle bitesize chunks. You'll also find many of my other playlists and great resources from other English teachers, as well as super Maths and Science teachers too.

My videos are free when you sign up at **www.tuitionkit.com/bruffsentme** using the code **"Bruffsentme"** and that code will also give you a **20%** discount on all the other material on the site for all your core GCSE subject revision.

To get a flavour for how TuitionKit's great features will help you revise, go to: **www.tuitionkit.com** and sign up for your free 48 hour trial. Remember all my videos will always be free and advert-free too, so head over to TuitionKit and get a step closer to the grades you deserve!

All the best with your studies.

Mr. Bruff

Paper 1: Shakespeare and the 19th-Century Novel

Paper 1 assesses your knowledge of one Shakespeare play and one 19th-century novel. Your teacher will select the texts that you are studying from the following:

Shakespeare
'Julius Caesar'
'Macbeth'
'Much Ado About Nothing'
'Romeo and Juliet'
'The Merchant of Venice'
'The Tempest'

19th-Century Novels
'A Christmas Carol' by Charles Dickens
'Frankenstein' by Mary Shelley
'Great Expectations' by Charles Dickens
'Jane Eyre' by Charlotte Brontë
'Pride and Prejudice' by Jane Austen
'The Sign of Four' by Sir Arthur Conan Doyle
'The Strange Case of Dr Jekyll and Mr Hyde' by Robert Louis Stevenson

In this guide, we shall look at examples from most of the above set texts.

The exam length is 1 hour, 45 minutes, and the paper is marked out of 64:

- 30 marks are available for Section A
- 4 marks are available for your spelling, punctuation and grammar in Section A.
- 30 marks are available for Section B

You should spend around 50 minutes on each section and an additional 5 minutes checking Section A for technical accuracy.

This is a closed book examination, which means that you are not allowed to take copies of your exam texts into the exam. There will, however, be extracts provided in the exam for you to analyse.

The paper 1 extracts will be around 10-20 lines in length and will be printed in the question paper. You will be asked to analyse the extracts and then refer to the wider text. Bearing in mind that this is a closed book exam, you will need to memorise key quotations from the text as part of your revision. Check out my revision songs playlist at www.youtube.com/mrbruff for an easy way to memorise key quotations!

Memorising Quotations
When it comes to memorising quotations, it is essential to select quotations which apply to a broad range of themes and topics. For example, consider the opening line of 'Pride and Prejudice':

> *It is a truth universally acknowledged, that a single man in possession of a good fortune, must be in want of a wife.*

This is an excellent quotation to memorise, as it lends itself to so many topics: attitudes to women, attitudes to men, the importance of marriage, different views of love, the use of narrative voice, etc. In fact, there is almost no occasion where this quotation could not be used in an exam answer. These are the quotations you need to find—ones that can be applied to all areas of the text.

The best way to find these quotations is to first write out all the major themes that a text contains. With 'Pride and Prejudice', that list might look something like this:

- Genre: romance and satire
- Context of 19th-century England
- Attitudes to women
- Attitudes to men
- Attitudes to love and marriage
- Attitudes to class
- Importance of setting
- Importance of the title
- Austen's use of structure

Once you have listed the major themes of a text (which should be the areas you are studying in school), you should look for quotations that apply to as many of these as possible. You can create a table like the one below:

THEME	QUOTATION	HOW IT APPLIES
Genre: romance and satire	'It is a truth universally acknowledged, that a single man in possession of a good fortune, must be in want of a wife'.	This is a tongue-in-cheek, satirical comment used to mock contemporary attitudes to marriage.
Context of 19th-century England	'It is a truth universally acknowledged, that a single man in possession of a good fortune, must be in want of a wife'.	Austen uses this quotation to mock the prevalent attitude in Georgian England that all rich men must be married because of their wealth.
Attitudes to women	'It is a truth universally acknowledged, that a single man in possession of a good fortune, must be in want of a wife'.	This quotation suggests that women are an object to be sought.
Attitudes to men	'It is a truth universally acknowledged, that a single man in possession of a good fortune, must be in want of a wife'.	It suggests that what men want, men get.
Attitudes to love and marriage	'It is a truth universally acknowledged, that a single man in possession of a good fortune, must be in want of a wife'.	Suggests that marriage is for wealth and status rather than love. Also suggests that money, rather than love, makes a person marriage material.
Attitudes to class	'It is a truth universally acknowledged, that a single man in possession of a good fortune, must be in want of a wife'.	Suggests that riches and wealth make a man good marriage material. Highlights attitudes to class.
Setting		
Importance of the title	'It is a truth universally acknowledged, that a single man in possession of a good fortune, must be in want of a wife'.	Links to prejudice in the title—prejudice towards those with money for no other reason than that they are wealthy.
Austen's use of structure	'It is a truth universally acknowledged, that a single man in possession of a good fortune, must be in want of a wife'.	By using this as the opening line, it highlights just how important this notion is to our understanding of the rest of the novel.

As you can see, the quotation fits almost all of the themes. As it doesn't easily fit into the theme of 'setting', I would then begin to look for a good quotation that applies to setting. So, by memorising just two quotations, I am able to give a quotation for any possible question in the exam. Try to fill in a table for your own set texts—email it to me at info@mrbruff.com and perhaps I will include it in future editions of this guide!

Linking Characters to Themes

What if the question in the exam is based upon the presentation of Mr Collins? How would I use my memorised quotation now? Students often panic when the characters named in exam questions seem to be minor, obscure or unimportant. The key thing to remember here is that all characters relate to themes so, when you are preparing for the exams, a tip is to link these characters to themes.

The writer (in this case, Jane Austen) has a number of themes and messages that she is exploring in her novel, and she uses characters to explore these themes. Let's take the rather obscure character of Mr Collins. At first glance, he might seem to be nothing more than a comic interlude in a novel that is otherwise quite serious. However, if we look at Mr Collins in light of the themes we've identified, we can see that he plays three major theme-linked roles:

1. Mr Collins is used to highlight the necessity of marriage for the Bennett daughters.

It is Mr Collins who is so rude as to mention the income that is available to the Bennet family after Mr Bennet's death. Mr Bennet's income of £2,000 a year, along with his house, would go to Mr Collins. Mrs Bennet would have to live off the 'one thousand pounds in the 4 per cents'. What does this mean? Well, with Mr Bennet's income entailed to Mr Collins, all that would be left is the interest on Mrs Bennet's £5,000 marriage settlement, which would equate to £200 a year. Of this, Elizabeth could expect an equal daughterly share of a fifth, leaving her with just £40 a year if she were not to marry before her father's death. This helps the reader to understand the necessity of marriage for the Bennet girls. The reader also has greater a respect for the strength of Elizabeth's convictions in refusing both Collins and Darcy. If the sisters fail to marry before their father's death, they will have a similar allowance to that of a farm labourer! Therefore, Mr Collins links to the themes of marriage, women and men.

2. Mr Collins is used as a satirical attack on class.

There are many hilarious sides to Mr Collins, but my favourite has to be his obsession with the fact that 'the chimney-piece alone [at Rosings] had cost eight hundred pounds'. This is a ridiculous point, made even more humorous for its regular repetition. Similarly, the way in which Lady Catherine seems to feature so heavily in Mr Collins's life is laughable. That Lady Catherine had 'vouchsafed to suggest…some shelves in the closet up stairs' in Mr Collins's house is ridiculous. However, behind these passages are the serious issues of undeserved respect for the higher classes and an obsession with wealth.

Austen's novel can be seen as a scathing criticism of class-based snobbery, society's expectations of women and attitudes to marriage. The genius of the writer is to disperse these themes into a very comic tale. As a result, readers understand the point but also enjoy themselves whilst they are reading. Austen is like that funny teacher at school who manages to make you laugh and get great grades at the same time.

3. Mr Collins is used to criticise the patriarchal society in which Austen was writing.

If the life of a woman in Austen's era is unfair, it is also unavoidable. In chapter 13, Mr Bennet reminds his daughters that Mr Collins has a right 'when I am dead...to turn you all out of this house as soon as he pleases'. What Mr Bennet refers to in this chapter is the act of entailment.

As the Bennets were a rich family, Mr Bennet's father entailed his property. This means that the entire wealth went to one person—the eldest son. That way, the wealth and property would remain strong and undiluted. What does this mean? Well, if the property had *not* been entailed and Mr Bennet's father had had lots of sons, their inheritance would have been divided into such small amounts that it would not have counted for much at all.

Because Mr Bennet's father entailed the property, Mr Bennet as the eldest son inherited everything. This tradition passes on to future generations, too. We learn that Mr Collins, the nearest male heir, is 'a distant relation' on Mr Bennet's patriarchal side of the family, despite the difference in surname. (Men changing their surnames was not uncommon in Georgian times. Austen's brother Edward changed his surname to Knight when he inherited a property from relations called Knight. In 'Emma', Frank Weston also changed his surname to Churchill when his rich childless uncle offered to raise him.) The big point here is that women were seen as so inferior that they were not recognised in entailment law. This is further explained in chapter 50:

> When first Mr. Bennet had married, economy was held to be perfectly useless; for, of course, they were to have a son. This son was to join in cutting off the entail, as soon as he should be of age, and the widow and younger children would by that means be provided for. Five daughters successively entered the world, but yet the son was to come; and Mrs. Bennet, for many years after Lydia's birth, had been certain that he would. This event had at last been despaired of, but it was then too late to be saving. Mrs. Bennet had no turn for economy, and her husband's love of independence had alone prevented their exceeding their income.

An estate did not have to be entailed, as we see with Lady Catherine's estate, which will be inherited by her daughter. However, once an estate was entailed, there was no room for females to inherit anything. This left many women in a very tough situation—they simply had to marry a rich man to maintain their lifestyle.

So, there we have it: Mr Collins is quite important after all! Why not try linking all the major and minor characters in the text that you are studying to at least one of its major themes? After mapping out the key themes of a text, try to find a small number of quotations that apply to as many of the themes as possible. Finally, link all characters to the themes/meanings they convey. If you know your text well, there is no way you can be shocked by something unexpected in the exam.

Assessment Objectives

The assessment objectives for this exam paper are:

AO1: Read, understand and respond to texts. Students should be able to:

- maintain a critical style and develop an informed personal response
- use textual references, including quotations, to support and illustrate interpretations.

AO2: Analyse the language, form and structure used by a writer to create meanings and effects, using relevant subject terminology where appropriate.

AO3: Show understanding of the relationships between texts and the contexts in which they were written.

AO4: Use a range of vocabulary and sentence structures for clarity, purpose and effect, with accurate spelling and punctuation.

This table contains public sector information licensed under the Open Government Licence v3.0.

The assessment objectives for both papers 1 and 2 are weighted, and this means that some have more importance than others:

	Paper 1	Paper 2	Overall
AO1	15%	22.5%	37.5%
AO2	15%	27.5%	42.5%
AO3	7.5%	7.5%	15%
AO4	2.5%	2.5%	5%
Total	40%	60%	100%

This table contains public sector information licensed under the Open Government Licence v3.0.

In simple terms, the greatest focus should be your ability to read, understand and respond to texts as well as your analysis of language, structure and form. This means that writing about context should be present but not overly focused upon. I will explore each of these in detail throughout this guide.

Understanding your Mark

The mark scheme is divided into six levels for both Section A and B of this exam. Level 6 (26-30 marks) is distinguished by three key areas:

1. Exploration of task, text and effect on reader
2. Conceptualised response to task and text, integrating knowledge of context
3. Analysis of writer's use language, structure and form

There are three key points to make here:

1. Top marks can only be achieved by those who analyse language, structure **and** form.
2. It is important to make detailed links between the context(s) and the question.
3. Students aiming for top marks will present a well-structured argument.

> **Let's look at those points in detail. As they apply to both literature papers, what I am about to explain applies to the entirety of this revision guide.**

AO2: LANGUAGE, STRUCTURE AND FORM

Before we look at an example analysis of language, structure and form, it's worth reviewing the difference between these three areas of analysis:

Language refers to vocabulary. This is the simplest line of analysis and the one which most students write about first. Whether you are picking out similes and metaphors or just words or phrases that seem important, it's all language analysis.

Structure refers to the organisation of a text. In the 19th century, the German novelist Gustav Freytag proposed that all five-act plays follow the same format:

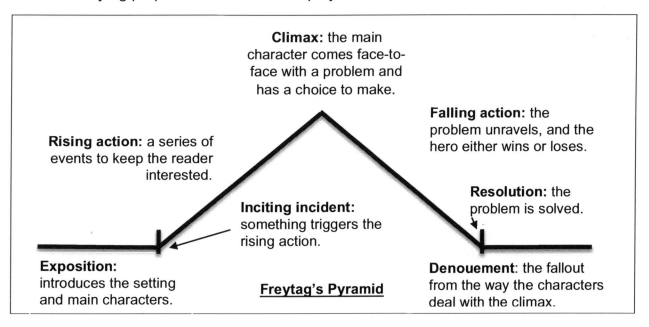

Climax: the main character comes face-to-face with a problem and has a choice to make.

Falling action: the problem unravels, and the hero either wins or loses.

Rising action: a series of events to keep the reader interested.

Resolution: the problem is solved.

Inciting incident: something triggers the rising action.

Exposition: introduces the setting and main characters.

Freytag's Pyramid

Denouement: the fallout from the way the characters deal with the climax.

In the literature exams, consider the structure of the extract and also the structure in relation to where that extract occurs in a text. Where is an extract placed in the text? Why is this important? Is there anything else that this shows us about characters and relationships?

Form refers to the writer following particular rules about the organisation of a text. Does the writer stick to the rules or break them? What does this show us about the writer's attitudes?

You will read an analysis of structure and form in the example responses in this guide. Before this, my whole-hearted advice is to look for points related to structure and form and make these first. Remember that the examiner will mark hundreds of papers. Most students will be writing about language, so for you to stand out and be recognised as perceptive, you need to make points that most students don't notice.

AO3: CONTEXT

Integrating your knowledge of context into your response is rewarded under AO3, and you should consider its effect not only on the contemporary audience but also the modern audience.

The term context can be understood in a variety of ways and will vary depending upon which text you are studying. Context can mean:

- When the text was written
- When and where the text is set
- Literary context and genre
- Or responses from different audiences.

Let's begin by considering the events and circumstances surrounding when a text was written.

Example of When and Where a Text is Set

Often, a writer will set their text in a different place to that in which he or she lives. Why do they do this? Sometimes, there are numerous reasons.

Let's begin by exploring Shakespeare's choice of a foreign setting for 'Romeo and Juliet'. Although many students assume that Shakespeare created the storylines of his plays, the truth is that it was often someone else who came up with the original plot. With Shakespeare plays, settings often reflect the source of a text. William Shakespeare sets 'Romeo and Juliet' in Verona, Italy, and this reflects the original story by the Italian writer Matteo Bandello (1480-1562), who created what we now know as 'Romeo and Juliet'. Bandello wrote the short story 'Giullette e Romeo', supposedly based on a true-life story that had taken place in his home country of Italy. In 1562, the English poet Arthur Brooke translated the short story into a poem (along with some small plot changes that affected minor characters such as the nurse and the friar). Brooke died a year after publication and the now classic tale was picked up by the English novelist William Painter, who adapted it into a novel entitled 'The Palace of

Pleasure' (1567). Finally, around the year 1590, William Shakespeare adapted the story for the stage, writing the play 'Romeo and Juliet'. In the years that followed, the play would become one of the best-known stories in the world.

So, it is probable that Shakespeare set 'Romeo and Juliet' in Italy because that is where the story originated. Also, the setting of Italy makes sense for the story—Italy was known as a romantic city, just as Paris is today. The streets are narrow, which creates a perfect intense setting for street fights; and the weather is hot, which will raise the tension and violence in the characters as their 'blood runs hot'. But what if Shakespeare is using the play to criticise elements of Elizabethan England?

The play can be read as a scathing criticism of Catholicism, as England had only just become a protestant nation. Perhaps Shakespeare felt it would be too controversial and risky to criticise Catholicism in his native country.

'Romeo and Juliet' can also be seen as a criticism of the English ritual of arranged marriage that was prevalent in the upper classes. Once again, perhaps Shakespeare did not wish to openly attack the conventions of his own country, so he detached it from England through its foreign setting. When Capulet calls his daughter a 'wretch' for refusing to marry Paris, Shakespeare is clearly pointing an accusatory finger at English fathers. In the 1500s, arranged marriages were normal for upper-class families when parents to choose whom their children married. Once again, Shakespeare uses a foreign setting to distance himself slightly from open criticism of Elizabethan England.

Similarly, 'The Merchant of Venice' is set in Venice, another foreign setting. Why might that be? Just like 'Romeo and Juliet', we have a story which Shakespeare did not himself create. The 14th-century writer Ser Giovanni wrote 'Il Pecorone' way before Shakespeare was born. This story tells of a rich young man who travels to Belmont and meets a rich widow. To win her over, he borrows money from a Jewish moneylender, which is ultimately paid for with a pound of flesh! Yes, it seems clear that one explanation for the Venetian setting is the fact that the story originated there. It also, like 'Romeo and Juliet', ties neatly into the plot. In Elizabethan England, Venice was a key trading centre: exotic goods were traded in the city, which was home to the explorer Marco Polo, so Venice is a great setting for a story where trade is essential.

It is also possible that Shakespeare set the play in Venice to distance himself slightly from the criticism of England that we find within the play. 'The Merchant of Venice' contains many themes, one of which is the treatment of Jews. In Shakespeare's time, Jews had been banished from England. One interpretation is that Shakespeare uses the play to attack the unjust treatment of the Jews. When Shylock asks, 'If you prick us do we not bleed?', it is easy to hear the voice of Shakespeare challenging his audience about their racist attitudes.

Whatever conclusions we draw, it is important to ask ourselves *where is the text set?* and *why is this important?*

You can buy Mr Bruff's guides to both Shakespeare plays at www.mrbruff.com

So why is Context so Important?

Now you understand some of the ways in which we can study context, let's look at how we can use it to inform our understanding.

At GCSE, relevant contextual factors often revolve around attitudes to gender, religion, marriage and love. Understanding these factors helps us to understand a text so much better. For example, at first glance, Act 1, Scene 3 of 'Romeo and Juliet' seems to be a simple comic scene but, when we understand contextual attitudes to women and marriage, it becomes clear that it is so much more.

Act 1, Scene 3 offers a welcome dose of comedy to the play. The nurse is a fantastic character with a bawdy, sexual sense of humour, and she is all-out slapstick in this scene. Perhaps the funniest part of this scene is where she recounts a story from Juliet's childhood:

> *For even the day before, she broke her brow: And then my husband—God be with his soul! A' was a merry man—took up the child: 'Yea,' quoth he, 'dost thou fall upon thy face? Thou wilt fall backward when thou hast more wit.*

After telling this story, the nurse, proving she is a forgetful woman, repeats the whole thing once more. The juxtaposition of the uninhibited nurse with the reserved Lady Capulet and Juliet makes the comic effect even more powerful.

However, this scene also offers an insight into the role of women in Shakespeare's time. In nurse's story, the baby Juliet falls over onto her face, and the nurse's husband remarked 'Thou wilt fall backward when thou comest to age'. The meaning of this line is clear: when you grow into a woman, you will fall onto your back to have sex. To a modern audience, this line may seem shocking—the nurse's husband is talking to a baby girl about the sexual future that awaits her. However, an Elizabethan audience would see nothing odd here.

In Shakespeare's time, women were seen as little more than mothers and objects of male desire. To this purpose, most girls were denied anything beyond a basic schooling. It was more common for upper-class families like Juliet's to hire tutors to teach their children. Even then, the prospects for educated women were very slim. Women could not enter any profession or even vote; instead, they were prepared for domestic lives. Upper-class girls were therefore taught how to cook, sew, play instruments and do anything else that appeared to make domestic life more attractive. The only option for a girl was therefore to get married and to run the household.

Today, women have no need to marry, but a failure to find a husband in Shakespeare's time meant a desperate life. Females could only survive through the men who provided for them. As children, a girl would rely on her father for financial support and protection. When married, this responsibility passed on to the husband. It was almost unheard of not to marry. If a girl did not marry, there were only two other options available: become a nun or become a prostitute. This shocking contextual detail helps up to see the situation Juliet is in. With this in mind, we can see that the nurse's husband was right: Juliet (and all girls of the time) was fated to end up being married to a man.

At the time 'Romeo and Juliet' was written, it was illegal to marry without parental consent. Juliet's mother and father want her to marry Paris, an eligible bachelor. It is an example of dramatic irony (where the audience know more than the characters on the stage) that we already know Juliet is fated to be with Romeo, not Paris.

As you can see, it is only through our understanding of context that we are able to fully appreciate the meaning of this scene.

AO1: A WELL-STRUCTURED ARGUMENT
a. PEE Paragraphs

I always recommend structuring your ideas in the PEE paragraph format. What does this mean? Let me explain:

P: Point
Answer the question in one sentence. Be sure to use the wording of the question to show the examiner that you are clearly answering the question.

E: Evidence
Find a quotation from the text that proves your point. Ideally, the quotation should be short and embedded into your sentence (so that the quotations read fluently as if it they are part of your sentence).

E: Explain
This is the most important part of the paragraph. Explain HOW your chosen quotation proves your point.

Let's look at a sample answer and break it into its PEE components:

Point: Shakespeare presents love as a religious and sacred experience.

Evidence: We see this through Shakespeare's use of language when Romeo continually uses religious imagery to explain his feelings to Juliet. He calls Juliet a 'holy shrine', which suggests that Juliet is a deity. Romeo also professes that he himself is a 'pilgrim'—someone on a religious journey to visit a sacred site.

Explain: This extended metaphor continues throughout the extract and is used by Shakespeare to suggest that Romeo and Juliet's love is pure, holy and sacred.

As you can see, it is vital that you know your set text in detail. Not only should you study the text in class, but you should read it yourself at home, perhaps looking for points about structure and form. In a closed book exam, there is no way you can achieve top marks without knowing your text thoroughly. Opinion varies but, as a teacher, I might have read and taught a text ten times, and I still find different points each time I read it.

At the very least, read your texts twice. Search online for free audiobook versions and listen to them whilst tidying your room (if you ever do such a thing!).

b. Organising your Paragraphs

When analysing a text, most students are able to pick out a few different ideas. However, many students write exam answers that consist of four or five disjointed ideas that bear no relation to each other.

Consider the first answer to the following Shakespeare question:

Example Response for Section A: Shakespeare's 'Romeo and Juliet'

Read the following extract from Act 1, Scene 5 of 'Romeo and Juliet' and then answer the questions. At this point in the play Romeo and Juliet have just met.

ROMEO
If I profane with my unworthiest hand,
This holy shrine; the gentle fine is this;
My lips, two blushing pilgrims, ready stand
To smooth that rough touch with a tender kiss.
JULIET
Good pilgrim, you do wrong your hand too much,
Which mannerly devotion shows in this;
For saints have hands that pilgrims' hands do touch,
And palm to palm is holy palmers' kiss.
ROMEO
Have not saints lips, and holy palmers too?
JULIET
Ay, pilgrim, lips that they must use in prayer.
ROMEO
O, then, dear saint, let lips do what hands do;
They pray, grant thou, lest faith turn to despair.
JULIET
Saints do not move, though grant for prayers' sake.
ROMEO
Then move not, while my prayer's effect I take.

Explore how Shakespeare presents attitudes towards love:

a) In this extract

b) In the play as a whole.

[30 marks] A04 [4 marks]

EXTRACT FROM A 'GOOD' SAMPLE ANSWER

In this extract, Shakespeare uses language to suggest that love is a spiritual and Godly emotion. We see this through his use of language when Romeo continually uses religious imagery when explaining his feelings to Juliet. He calls Juliet a 'holy shrine', which suggests that Juliet is a deity. Romeo also professes that he himself is a 'pilgrim'—someone on a religious journey to visit a sacred site. This extended metaphor continues throughout the extract and is used by Shakespeare to suggest that the love felt by Romeo and Juliet is pure, holy and sacred.

Shakespeare uses form to convey the importance of the love between Romeo and Juliet. The combined conversation between the two joins together to complete a perfect sonnet. A sonnet is a form of love poetry, which has fourteen lines of iambic pentameter, with the rhyme scheme ABAB CDCD EFEF GG. Shakespeare's employment of form is here used to symbolise that the couple are perfect for each other and they complete each other. Only when united together do their words create a sonnet, symbolising how they can only find true love when joined together. The audience would feel delighted that these two, both so clearly unhappy with the way their lives are heading, have found perfect happiness.

In the wider context of the play, Shakespeare presents love as a very sexual experience. We see this in Act 1 when Romeo laments that Rosaline would not 'ope her lap to saint seducing gold'. Romeo is here explaining that Rosaline would not have sex with him, even when offered money. This suggests that love is a very sexual experience.

Whilst this answer is quite sophisticated (particularly the points concerning form), it fails to come across as a well-constructed argument. There is no link between the three paragraphs; it reads as three totally different ideas: love as religious, love as perfect, love as sexual. To hit the top marks, you need to create a thread of argument that fits these points together. Rephrasing the answer in this way would then allow us to present a well-structured argument.

The example response on the next page illustrates a clear thread of discussion. It is, however, longer than anything a student would be able to write under timed exam conditions. It's been included as a teaching tool, particularly so that you can see examples of language, form, structure and context woven together in a thread of argument.

As you read, consider which bits you would use in an exam.

EXTRACT FROM A 'BETTER' SAMPLE ANSWER

Both in this extract and the wider play, Shakespeare presents love as all-encompassing, filling every aspect of life. To begin with, the extract is the inciting incident of the play when Romeo and Juliet first meet. This is important because it causes the conflict that leads to the deaths of Romeo and Juliet. Perhaps Shakespeare is showing the audience how love is not all positive, and the choices we make have clear consequences not just for ourselves, but for others as well.

Despite this, Shakespeare suggests that love is a spiritual and Godly emotion. We see this through Shakespeare's use of language where Romeo continually uses religious imagery; he calls Juliet a 'holy shrine', which suggests that Juliet is a deity. Romeo also professes that he is a 'pilgrim'—someone on a religious journey to visit a sacred site. This extended metaphor continues throughout the extract and is used by Shakespeare to suggest that Romeo and Juliet's love is pure, holy and sacred. This is the first time the audience has seen Romeo use such religious language and, as result, we are inclined to believe that he is genuinely in love. As the play is set in Italy, a very religious city, the use of religious language seems appropriate for the historical period.

Furthermore, we have the structural feature of mirroring when Juliet repeats Romeo's words (for example 'pilgrim'). Perhaps this shows us that she is naïve and following his lead, or it might show that her feelings for Romeo match his for her. Interestingly, when we consider male-female relationships of the time, this could also reflect how men were dominant and took the lead.

If the spiritual aspect of love is one side, the other side of love is the physical and sexual aspect, which is presented as being just as important by Shakespeare. Earlier in the play, Romeo laments how Rosaline will not 'ope her lap for saint seducing gold'. This line is ambiguous, but seems to suggest that Romeo had offered Rosaline payment in return for sexual gratification. Here, Shakespeare is presenting a different side to love—not only is it spiritual, but also physical. The message is clear: love is all-encompassing and all-consuming. The audience would note that two seemingly contrasting topics are used to discuss the theme of love, suggesting that in true love there is no contrast: all is united. At the time in which the play was written, arranged marriages were the norm between the middle and upper classes. An Elizabethan audience would therefore understand Shakespeare's message that true love transcends the conventions of society.

Finally, Shakespeare uses form to convey this all-encompassing nature of love. The combined conversation between the two in the extract joins together to complete a perfect sonnet. Shakespearean or Elizabethan sonnets are a form of love poetry that have fourteen lines of iambic pentameter with the rhyme scheme ABAB CDCD EFEF GG. Shakespeare's employment of form is here used to symbolise that the couple are perfect for each other, and that they complete each other. Only when united together do their words create a sonnet, symbolising how they can only find true love when joined together. The audience would feel delighted that these two, both so clearly unhappy with the way their lives are heading, have found perfect happiness. Perfect love, it seems clear, is the joined combination of spiritual and physical romance.

As you can see, I didn't have to do much to join my points together into one well-constructed argument. It just required a little thought. Throughout both literature papers, this is something you need to do to achieve the highest marks available. When we get to the poetry, there are some poems that compare better than others simply because they have a strong line of argument between them.

Many students fail to realise that every exam question can elicit a conceptualised, well-argued response. When writing exam questions, examiners have to spend a lot of time thinking about the possible responses. You too must give yourself at least a few minutes of planning time to think about a line of argument in the exam.

RELATING YOUR POINTS TO THE TEXT AS A WHOLE
The above response is an example of a top-band response, which not only has a thread of discussion but also analyses language, structure and form in detail.

Remember, this is a closed book exam. Because of this, the bulk of your answer should focus on the given extract.

The exam question will also ask you to write about the theme's presentation in the text as a whole. There is no requirement to write an equal amount to your response to the extract. In fact, it is fine to write more about the extract and perhaps one good paragraph about the rest of the text. If you are inspired to write in more detail, here's an example response about the rest of the text:

THE REST OF THE TEXT

In Act 3, Scene 5, Shakespeare presents two contrasting views of love. To begin, Juliet and Romeo have had their first night together in bed. Shakespeare uses overexaggerated language to show just how in love they are. Juliet argues that the sun is not the sun but is, in fact 'some meteor that the sun exhales, to be to thee this night a torch-bearer'. She argues that the sun has fired out a meteor, which will be a light to guide Romeo on his way home to Mantua. This kind of passionate exaggeration is one of the conventions of courtly love. Courtly love is a historical concept that centres on two members of the nobility who secretly love each other. In literature, tales of courtly love always include examples of passionate exaggeration as well as imagery related to nature. As we can see in this quotation, Juliet includes both in her comments to Romeo. Shakespeare is here using the well-known conventions of courtly love to highlight just how much the couple love each other.

This loving relationship with Romeo is juxtaposed with the relationship Juliet has with Lord Capulet. Shakespeare uses structure, putting both relationships next to each other in one scene, to heighten the difference between the two.

The relationship between Juliet and her father is one in which he is possessive and controlling. In Act 3 Scene 5 Juliet refuses to do as her father orders, which is to marry Paris. He then insults her by calling her 'baggage'. This suggests that, just like a bag, she is a burden to him—a weight that weighs him down and an accessory. It suggests that she is his possession to do with as he pleases. Just like a bag, she is unimportant to him. Juliet would have been heartbroken to be called this, but an Elizabethan audience would have sided with her father. This is because in the 1500s, arranged marriages were normal for middle-class families. It was acceptable for parents to choose marriage partners, so the audience would have agreed that Juliet should follow her father's instruction. A modern audience would be outraged, as women's rights have moved on, and a modern viewer would believe that Juliet should be able to do as she pleases.

Note that context is assessed in the Shakespeare question, and so this response weaves in knowledge of context as a secondary factor to support other points. You can do this with section A or Section B or both. Be aware, however, that your analysis of language, form and structure and your knowledge of the texts are worth more marks, so these AOs should be your main focus. Buy 'Mr Bruff's Guide to 'Romeo and Juliet'' at www.mrbruff.com

Example Response for Section A: Shakespeare's 'Macbeth'

Read the following extract from Act 1, Scene 1 of 'Macbeth' and then answer the questions.

Thunder and lightning. Enter three Witches.

FIRST WITCH
When shall we three meet again
In thunder, lightning, or in rain?

SECOND WITCH
When the hurlyburly's done,
When the battle's lost and won.

THIRD WITCH
That will be ere the set of sun.

FIRST WITCH
Where the place?

SECOND WITCH
Upon the heath.

Third Witch
There to meet with Macbeth.

FIRST WITCH
I come, Graymalkin!

SECOND WITCH
Paddock calls.

THIRD WITCH
Anon!

ALL
Fair is foul, and foul is fair:
Hover through the fog and filthy air.
Exeunt

Explore how Shakespeare presents the witches:

a) In this extract

b) In the play as a whole

[30 marks] A04 [4 marks]

EXAMPLE ANSWER

Because the extract is at the beginning of the play, it is part of the exposition (Freytag's pyramid), and Shakespeare's decision to introduce us to the witches from the outset shows that they are significant to the plot. The witches introduce the theme of the supernatural and, in Jacobean times, the witches would have been a big draw for audiences because there was a huge amount of interest (and belief) in witchcraft and the supernatural. King James I, Shakespeare's patron, was particularly interested in witches, having written a book on the subject ('Daemonologie'). It was also illegal to practise witchcraft—King James I of England was also King James VI of Scotland. He is estimated to be responsible for the burning of 4,000 alleged witches in Scotland. Believing in witches, he once took, according to contemporary accounts, 'great delight' in torturing a suspect. Beginning the play with this scene is therefore not only a good way to grab the interest of the audience but also of the king, an important source of revenue.

The curiosity of the audience is also aroused because we meet the witches when they have just finished doing something. The first lines of the play are: 'When shall we three meet again/In thunder, lightning, or in rain?' This prompts the curiosity of the audience. The interrogative with the reference to the weather also introduces a dark world full of confusion, and we associate the witches with evil, as they align themselves with bad weather.

The form used by the witches is trochaic tetrameter with stressed syllables followed by unstressed syllables. For example:

Fair is foul and foul is fair

The last stressed syllable 'fair' is not followed by a stressed syllable, which creates a frightening sense of finality: they are turning the world upside down, and we cannot stop it. The witches are the only characters in the play to speak in trochaic tetrameter (the other characters speak in either blank verse or prose); this heightens a sense of their otherworldliness and makes them stand out from the rest of the characters, emphasising their wickedness.

The witches also use alliteration with 'Fair is foul and foul is fair' to create a sinister mood to the play. This is because it draws the attention of the audience to the juxtaposition of the words themselves: everything that is good ('fair') is now bad ('foul') and everything that is bad is now good. This is emphasised through the use of rhyming couplets to create a fast pace. For example: 'Fair is foul and foul is fair/hover through the fog and the filthy air'. The rhyme continues the alliteration and develops the idea that this is a frightening, mysterious world where everything is turned upside down and the supernatural holds some power. The overall impression is that of a nursery rhyme but one that is much darker and evil. This would have been particularly frightening to the Jacobean audience although less frightening to a more cynical modern audience.

The witches' use of paradox also develops an atmosphere of confusion and tension. They talk about meeting again when a battle is both 'lost and won'. These contrasting adjectives create a sense of things being not what they seem: of appearance versus reality. This is very important for the rest of the play, as we see that many of the most important moments are based on this contrast. For example, in Act 1, Scene 5, the theme of appearance versus reality or confusion and opposites develops when Lady Macbeth scorns her husband's good qualities (he has too much 'human kindness') before calling on the spirits to 'unsex' her so that she can do a man's work and kill King Duncan. To her, just as to the witches, goodness is a bad thing. In this scene, we see evidence of 'Fair is foul and foul is fair', as the rest of this scene involves the fair Lady Macbeth foully invoking evil spirits to help her to achieve her goals. This 'foul' behaviour is attractive ('fair') to the witches. For Shakespeare's audience, dedicating oneself to evil and calling on demonic spirits would have been very powerful. Lady Macbeth crosses over to the dark side and there is evidence to suggest that she has, in fact, become possessed. Later in the play we see her sleepwalking, unable to sleep properly and talking to herself. These are all symptoms that Shakespeare's audience would have understood as being possessed by demons.

The animal imagery in Act 1, Scene 1 with 'Graymalkin' and 'Paddock', the witches' familiars, confirms to the audience that the witches are evil. This use of animal imagery to represent evil is extended to develop the theme of appearance versus reality at the end of the Act 1, Scene 5. Lady Macbeth has decided that Duncan is to be murdered and she tells Macbeth him to 'look like the innocent flower, but be the serpent under't'. Here we have the metaphor of concealment, confusion and hidden identity. The serpent connotes the serpent in the story of Adam and Eve, and this develops the idea of cunning and evil, especially as, like Eve, Lady Macbeth influences her husband for the worse.

Note that there is no introduction and conclusion, because you are not asked to write an essay. Buy 'Mr Bruff's Guide to 'Macbeth'' at www.mrbruff.com

Example Response for Section A: Shakespeare's 'The Tempest'

Read the following extract from Act 1 Scene 2 of 'The Tempest' where we meet Caliban for the first time. Then answer the questions.

PROSPERO
Abhorred slave,
Which any print of goodness wilt not take,
Being capable of all ill! I pitied thee,
Took pains to make thee speak, taught thee each hour
One thing or other. When thou didst not, savage,
Know thine own meaning, but wouldst gabble like
A thing most brutish, I endow'd thy purposes
With words that made them known. But thy vile race,
Though thou didst learn, had that in't which good natures
Could not abide to be with. Therefore wast thou
Deservedly confined into this rock,
Who hadst deserved more than a prison.

CALIBAN
You taught me language, and my profit on't
Is, I know how to curse. The red plague rid you
For learning me your language!

PROSPERO
Hag-seed, hence!
Fetch us in fuel. And be quick, thou'rt best,
To answer other business. Shrug'st thou, malice?
If thou neglect'st or dost unwillingly
What I command, I'll rack thee with old cramps,
Fill all thy bones with aches, make thee roar
That beasts shall tremble at thy din.

Explore how Shakespeare presents Prospero ability to control others:

a) In this extract

b) In the play as a whole

[30 marks] A04 [4 marks]

EXAMPLE ANSWER

If we analyse the extract using Freytag's pyramid, this moment is used as part of the rising action of the play to present Prospero's relationship with Caliban. It provides the audience with the opportunity to meet Caliban and form their own judgements about Prospero's relationship with him.

The two characters represent the relationship between the coloniser and the colonised. Prospero, the coloniser, insults Caliban with a range of terms of address, calling him '[a]bhorred slave', 'hag-seed' and 'malice'. Prospero is full of contempt for Caliban, and the strength of these insults implies that his opinion will not change. His attitude appears to be rather unfair, considering that Caliban cannot help being the offspring of the witch Sycorax.

Prospero also positions himself as the one who has been betrayed. He implies that Caliban, the colonised, should be grateful to him, stating that when he first arrived on the island, he 'pitied' Caliban and '[t]ook pains' to teach him to 'speak' English as Caliban 'wouldst gabble like/A thing most brutish'. We have the colonial attitude that it was not worth leaning Caliban's language, but it was acceptable to impose English on Caliban. The length of Prospero's speech also reflects his absolute power, and this might symbolise contemporary attitudes in which no-one questioned the right of colonisers to take land and impose their values on the indigenous populations of America and Ireland.

Caliban's response shows his defiance and ironic insight:

You taught me language, and my profit on't
Is, I know how to curse.

Caliban uses language as a weapon to 'curse' Prospero. The noun 'profit' reminds the reader of Stephano and Trinculo thinking about how they can exhibit Caliban in a freak show and make money out of him. In this instance, however, Caliban is the person who, through language, gains the profit or advantage of being able to fight back. Like Prospero, Caliban speaks in blank verse, which is often used by high-status characters. This implies that he sees himself as the true owner of the island and that he will not allow himself to be oppressed.

Prospero is only able to control Caliban through magic which, with 'cramps' and 'aches' utilises physical torture. The 'cramps' are 'old', implying that this has happened before. This makes the audience appreciate the strength of Caliban's personality, as he can be made to do what Prospero wants, but Prospero cannot break his spirit.

Prospero also uses a lot of imperatives (direct orders) such as 'Hag-seed, hence! /Fetch us in fuel', which emphasises his higher status and Caliban's position of 'slave'.

Elsewhere in the play, Prospero uses magic to terrify the 'three men of sin', Alonso, Ferdinand and Antonio, when he has Ariel appears in the guise of a harpy. The educated courtiers, who will have studied Greek mythology, will know that a harpy torments evil people and carries their souls away to be punished by the gods. The courtiers would have been terrified by the sight of the avenging supernatural creature (as we would, today!), and the audience would have been thrilled.

Prospero uses Ariel's magic powers to make the men repent, telling them that they are 'unfit to live'. In his monologue, Ariel uses the idea of 'Destiny' against the courtiers, stating 'I and my fellows/Are ministers of fate'. Elizabethans and Jacobeans believed that fate controlled people's lives and that their destiny was pre-determined. Because of the contemporary belief in fate, the impact of Ariel's speech on the courtiers is terrifying, because they believe that they are doomed to divine retribution and that therefore there can be no hope for them in the afterlife.

Once Prospero has confronted the men with their crimes, he continues to use the disguised Ariel's magic to introduce the theme of repentance and forgiveness. He tells Alonso that his fate can only be averted through 'heart's sorrow' (repentance) and 'a clear life ensuing' (an unblemished life from here on). This contrasts with the 'monstrous, monstrous' realisation by Alonso of the enormity of his crime against Prospero and successfully makes him repent.

Elsewhere in the play, magic appears to be used to celebrate the hand-fasting of Ferdinand and Miranda when Prospero uses his spirits to create a masque. However, Prospero is attempting to control Ferdinand by showing him what can be achieved through magic. The expectations of the time were that a hand-fasting must be solemnised with a church wedding before consummation could take place. Prospero therefore threatens Ferdinand with curses to make him comply, warning him that if he breaks Miranda's 'virgin-knot' before their church wedding, nothing 'sweet' will follow. Part of the purpose of the masque in this scene is to show off Prospero's powers when he conjures up the goddesses. This in turn is more likely to make Ferdinand obey him.

Buy 'Mr Bruff's Guide to The Tempest" at www.mrbruff.com

Does the Quality of my Writing Matter?
AO4 is assessed in Section A of both literature exams. Four marks are available for AO4, which doesn't seem much. If your result is borderline, however, those four marks could tip you into a higher band.

To gain full marks for AO4, you should achieve consistent accuracy in spelling and punctuation. You must also use sentence structures and vocabulary to clearly express meaning. Let's spend some time looking at the importance of spelling, punctuation and grammar.

TECHNICAL ACCURACY
The grammar and punctuation marks below are the ones that you will need to focus on the most in your literature exams. Explanations of all the punctuation marks in much more detail are in the ebook 'Mr Bruff's Guide to Grammar' at www.mrbruff.com or available in paperback on Amazon.

Sentence Variety

Your ability to control sentences is part of the mark scheme; the most common sentences that you are most likely to use in the literature exam are:

Simple Sentences

Simple sentences contain a subject and a verb.

Example: *He laughed.*

In this example, we have a verb (in this case, an action): 'laughed'. If we ask ourselves who or what is 'doing' the verb, the answer is 'he'. Therefore, 'he' is the subject. Simple sentences are mostly, but not always, short.

It's possible to add adjectives and adverbs to simple sentences: *The tired old man walked slowly along the ancient stone path.* Although this sentence is longer, it still only contains one subject and one verb: 'man' and 'walked', so it is a simple sentence.

Compound Sentences

Compound sentences join two independent clauses (that look like simple sentences) with one of the following words, called co-ordinating conjunctions:

> **F**or
> **A**nd
> **N**or
> **B**ut
> **O**r
> **Y**et
> **S**o

You might have heard about them in school as 'FANBOYS'. (The conjunction 'for' is a slightly old-fashioned word, used to mean 'because'.)

We usually have a comma before these conjunctions.

Example: *The man laughed, and his wife cried.*

Here we have two independent clauses:

> The man laughed (subject = man, verb = laughed)

> His wife cried (subject = wife, verb = cried).

All we've done is join them together with one of the FANBOYS conjunctions and added a comma.

Complex Sentences

Complex sentences have different (subordinating) conjunctions such as:

although
because
even if
if
while

Example: *I love you although you drive me crazy.*

If the subordinating conjunction is in the middle of the sentence, there is no comma. If the sentence starts with a subordinating conjunction, there is a comma:

Example: *Although you drive me crazy, I love you.*

Complex sentences are divided into two parts:

1. The part which makes sense on its own. We call this the main clause and it looks like a simple sentence. In the above example, the main clause is 'I love you'.

2. The part which does not make sense on its own. We call this the subordinate clause. In the example above, the subordinate clause begins with the subordinating conjunction 'although you drive me crazy'.

The above is just one example of many different types of complex sentence. Here are others:

Informative and entertaining, the popular book became a worldwide bestseller.

Exhausted but relieved, the students finally finished their GCSE exams

Straining with the effort, Grandma did a backflip.

Happily, the man whistled a tune.

Note how the comma always divides the main and subordinate clauses.

Compound-complex Sentences

A compound-complex sentence consists of a compound sentence (two independent clauses joined with a FANBOYS, or co-ordinating, conjunction) and at least one subordinate clause.

Example: *I bought this book because it looked useful, but now I am confused.*

Let's break it down:

'I bought this book' = independent clause

'because it looked useful' = subordinate clause

'but' = FANBOYS (co-ordinating) conjunction

'now I am confused' = independent clause

Capital Letters

Capital letters may seem to be very easy but, if you make mistakes with these apparently simple pieces of punctuation, then you will struggle to gain a high grade. There is little more off-putting and instantly recognisable to an examiner than the incorrect use of a capital letter.

You should use a capital letter for:

1. The start of a sentence e.g. *Today is the best day of my life.*

2. Names of people, brands, days of the week and months e.g. *Megan, Nike, Monday, January.*

3. Countries and cities e.g. *America, Plymouth.*

4. Languages and religions e.g. *French, Buddhist.*

5. Holidays e.g. *Christmas, Ramadan*

6. The first and significant words in a title need a capital e.g. *The Lord of the Rings.* In this example, the words 'of' and 'the' are not significant—they don't hold the meaning, so they are not capitalised.

7. The personal pronoun 'I' e.g. *Matt and I love reading.*

8. Abbreviations e.g. *BBC.*

Quotation Marks

These marks show the exact words that you are quoting from a text. Note that the full stop comes after the closing quotation mark. Example:

Alexander Pope said 'To err is human, to forgive divine'.

Brackets

You might use brackets in a literature exam to separate evidence so that the flow of your idea isn't interrupted. For example:

Romeo's semantic field of religion ('pilgrim', 'saints' and 'prayers') shows how perfect and holy their love is.

Ellipsis

When you are quoting, you might not want to copy a long sentence from the extract. Instead, use ellipsis to show what you have left out.

Here is an extract from 'Jane Eyre':

BEFORE ELLIPSIS:

I ought to forgive you, for you knew not what you did: while rending my heart-strings, you thought you were only uprooting my bad propensities.

Study how ellipsis is used in the following sentence:

AFTER ELLIPSIS:

Jane states: 'I ought to forgive you...you thought you were only uprooting my bad propensities'.

The ellipsis helps the reader to focus on the important remaining words that you will analyse.

The Apostrophe of Omission

This is the simplest type of apostrophe, used to show where letters or words have been taken out. Read the following example:

I didn't even know that spiders can bite.

Explanation: Here, we have shortened the words *did* and *not* into the word *didn't*. In doing so, we have taken out the letter *-o*, so we put an apostrophe of omission in its place to indicate this.

I would recommend developing a formal academic writing style by writing words in full instead of shortening them (especially if you are thinking of doing an A' level in English literature).

The Apostrophe of Possession

The apostrophe of possession shows us who or what owns something. For example:

Juliet's heart is broken.

Explanation: always ask yourself who or what the thing belongs to. Whatever the answer is, the apostrophe goes after that. For example, who does the heart belong to? The answer is *Juliet*, so the apostrophe goes after *Juliet*.

Commas

We have already looked at comma use with compound and complex sentences. Here is a summary of some other uses of the comma that might be handy:

1. Listing commas

This is the one everyone knows: we use commas to break up items in a list, except for between the last two items where we use the word 'and'. The comma is correct if it can be replaced with the word 'and' or 'or'.

> The four flavours of Starburst are orange, lemon, lime and apple.

2. To separate information connectives

In your literature exams, you will be using phrases like:

Furthermore, in addition, however, in contrast, to conclude, etc. to begin sentences. Separate these phrases with a comma. For example:

> To begin, 'Romeo and Juliet' is about two lovers.
>
> In addition, it is about family feuding.
>
> However, there is more to the play than that.

3. Bracketing commas (parenthetical commas)

This is my own personal favourite use of the comma, largely because it is a simple way of making your written work seem very impressive. Use commas instead of brackets:

Brackets	Bracketing commas
The nurse (a comic character) helps the couple.	The nurse, a comic character, helps the couple.

Both sentences make sense if we take the bit out between the bracketing commas, leaving us with:

> The nurse helps the couple.

Like brackets, the bracketing commas give us extra, unimportant information about the subject of the sentence—in the example, the nurse. There is a slight difference in meaning, however. With bracketing commas, the extra information is slightly more important.

Semicolons

a. With a compound sentence
In the literature exam, you might use semicolons to join two sentences that are of equal importance. A simple tip is to write a compound sentence and replace the FANBOYS (or co-ordinating) conjunction with a semicolon. This works better with 'so', 'and' and 'but'. Here are some before and after examples:

Compound sentence	With semicolon replacement
Romeo's heart was broken by Rosaline, and then he fell in love with Juliet.	Romeo's heart was broken by Rosaline; then he fell in love with Juliet.

Romeo fell in love with Juliet, so they secretly married.	Romeo fell in love with Juliet; they secretly married.
Romeo arrived at the tomb, but it was too late.	Romeo arrived at the tomb; it was too late.

Remember: semicolons can only be used to join two complete sentences.

b. With a conjunctive adverb
In the literature exam, you might also use a semicolon to introduce a conjunctive adverb that joins two sentences. Here are some of the most common conjunctive adverbs:

Consequently	Meanwhile	Similarly
Furthermore	Moreover	Still
However	Otherwise	Therefore
Indeed	Nevertheless	

Example of the semicolon with a conjunctive adverb:

> At first glance, 'Romeo and Juliet' appears to be about two lovers in Italy; however, some people say it's really a criticism of arranged marriages in England.

Colon

In the exam, you are more likely to use the colon in the following ways:

1. To show that the second half of a sentence is more important than the first.
Imagine a colon as a fanfare: it announces something important.

2. To introduce a long quotation:

> We see an embedded stage direction that tells the actor to take Juliet's hand when Romeo says: 'If I profane with my unworthiest hand,/This holy shrine'.

The forward slash punctuation mark / shows that in the original text, the next part of the quotation is on a new line.

Please note that it is a much higher order skill to take short quotations and to drop them into your own sentences.

Paper 1 Section B: the 19th-century Novel

Before we begin by looking at an example response to Mary Shelley's 'Frankenstein', let's put the novel into context.

Context of Mary Shelley's 'Frankenstein'

'Frankenstein' was written in the early 1800s, at a time of great social and historical change. In the 1760s, Jean Jacques Rousseau's 'Emile' explored the nature of education and human beings. In this text, the writer argues that humans are born harmless, and that it is society that makes people either good or bad. Today, we might call this the 'nature versus nurture' debate, and it is certainly one of the major themes in 'Frankenstein'.

The novel 'Frankenstein' is a horror text and, to make something truly horrific, it needs to tap into the fears of its readers; Shelley did this brilliantly. In order to create a truly terrifying book, Mary Shelley based the foundations of her tale on a recent scientific development that had been frightening the public: Galvanism.

Luigi Galvani was a scientist who experimented on dead animals with electricity. He found that the limbs of animals could be caused to spasm if touched with an electric current. Giovanni Aldini, Galvani's nephew, took these experiments one step further and tried them out on the body of a human being. In 1803, a man named George Foster murdered his wife and child and was hanged for the crime. Shortly after the hanging, Aldini took Foster's body and experimented on it with electricity. The results were detailed as follows:

> On the first application of the process to the face, the jaws of the deceased criminal began to quiver, and the adjoining muscles were horribly contorted, and one eye was actually opened. In the subsequent part of the process the right hand was raised and clenched, and the legs and thighs were set in motion'.

As you can see, there are similarities with the novel 'Frankenstein' where, in chapter 5, we read:

> By the glimmer of the half-extinguished light, I saw the dull yellow eye of the creature open; it breathed hard, and a convulsive motion agitated its limbs.

The similarities are uncanny—even down to the opening of just one eye! Mary Shelley bases the ideas in her novel on real-life events: the experimentation of electricity with dead bodies. This makes the novel terrifying, as contemporary readers would worry that what happens in the novel (the creature goes on an unstoppable murderous rampage) would happen in real life too. It could be argued that this is why the novel is still so popular. Today, we experiment with cloning, stem cell research and artificial intelligence. Behind it all is the fear that the results of our creation will overpower us, causing chaos and devastation.

Example Response for Section B: Mary Shelley's 'Frankenstein'

Explore how Shelley presents the creature and Frankenstein:

a) In this extract
b) In the novel as a whole

[30 marks]

"But it is true that I am a wretch. I have murdered the lovely and the helpless; I have strangled the innocent as they slept, and grasped to death his throat who never injured me or any other living thing. I have devoted my creator, the select specimen of all that is worthy of love and admiration among men, to misery; I have pursued him even to that irremediable ruin. There he lies, white and cold in death. You hate me; but your abhorrence cannot equal that with which I regard myself I look on the hands which executed the deed; think on the heart in which the imagination of it was conceived, and long for the moment when these hands will meet my eyes, when that imagination will haunt my thoughts no more.

"Fear not that I shall be the instrument of future mischief. My work is nearly complete. Neither yours nor any man's death is needed to consummate the series of my being, and accomplish that which must be done; but it requires my own. Do not think that I shall be slow to perform this sacrifice. I shall quit your vessel on the ice-raft which brought me thither, and shall seek the most northern extremity of the globe; I shall collect my funeral pile and consume to ashes this miserable frame, that its remains may afford no light to any curious and unhallowed wretch who would create such another as I have been. I shall die. I shall no longer feel the agonies which now consume me, or be the prey of feelings unsatisfied, yet unquenched. He is dead who called me into being; and when I shall be no more the very remembrance of us both will speedily vanish. I shall no longer see the sun or stars, or feel the winds play on my cheeks. Light, feeling, and sense will pass away; and in this condition must I find my happiness. Some years ago, when the images which this world affords first opened upon me, when I felt the cheering warmth of summer, and heard the rustling of the leaves and the warbling of the birds, and these were all to me, I should have wept to die; now it is my only consolation. Polluted by crimes, and tom by the bitterest remorse, where can I find rest but in death?

"Farewell! I leave you, and in you the last of human kind whom these eyes will ever behold. Farewell, Frankenstein! If thou wert yet alive, and yet cherished a desire of revenge against me, it would be better satiated in my life than in my destruction. But it was not so; thou didst seek my extinction that I might not cause greater wretchedness; and if yet, in some mode unknown to me, thou hast not ceased to think and feel, thou wouldst not desire against me a vengeance greater than that which I feel. Blasted as thou wert, my agony was still superior to thine; for the bitter sting of remorse will not cease to rankle in my wounds until death shall close them for ever.

"But soon," he cried, with sad and solemn enthusiasm, "I shall die, and what I now feel be no longer felt. Soon these burning miseries will be extinct. I shall ascend my funeral pile triumphantly, and exult in the agony of the torturing flames. The light of that conflagration will fade away; my ashes will be swept into the sea by the winds. My spirit will sleep in peace; or if it thinks, it will not surely think thus. Farewell."

He sprung from the cabin-window, as he said this, upon the ice-raft which lay close to the vessel. He was soon borne away by the waves and lost in darkness and distance.

The following answer was submitted by a student (who wishes to remain anonymous) for use in this book. It is an incredibly impressive analysis of language, form and structure.

EXAMPLE ANSWER

Throughout the novel, Shelley's use of language, structure and form cause the sympathies of the reader to alternate between Victor and the creature. In this extract, Shelley creates pathos for the creature by humanising him through his love of nature and the lyrical language that he uses. By making this passage the closing statement of the novel, Shelley leaves the reader with a lasting impression of the creature's inherent good nature, creating sympathy for the creature rather than Victor.

In this extract, Shelley constantly associates the creature with nature. The creature describes himself as missing the 'sun and stars', the feeling of 'the winds play on [his] cheeks', and the 'cheering warmth of summer'. This imagery is overwhelmingly positive, and the word 'play' connotes a childlike innocence and associates nature with the pure love and innocence a child feels before they are corrupted by the evils of the world. Through this, Shelley echoes ideas of Romanticism in that all children are born good and are corrupted by the world, ideas that Rousseau wrote about in the famous Romantic text 'Emile'. By associating the creature with this childish innocence, Shelley encourages the reader to feel sympathetic towards the creature and to believe that the crimes that he committed were because of the corrupting nature of man: they were not his own fault. Shelley uses this throughout the novel, for example, by giving the creature a diet of 'fruit and berries'. This also brings him closer to nature and thereby makes the reader sympathise with him.

Another way that Shelley makes the reader sympathise with the creature is through his use of language. In this passage, the creature speaks with lyrical eloquence, such as the use of hypotaxis in the sentence starting with 'some years ago…'. This creates a wistful and nostalgic tone, emphasising his love for nature, which creates sympathy for him, as it emphasises his humanity. Shelley contrasts this with the harsh, guttural short sentences frequently used by Victor throughout the novel, such as 'fiend!' and 'wretch!'. By presenting the creature as the more eloquent and better spoken of the two, the reader feels alienated from Victor's cruel language and therefore sympathises with the creature. Furthermore, Shelley's use of 'some years ago' reminds the reader of the tale that the creature told Victor in the mountains. This makes the reader remember that this is not the first time that the reader has heard lyrical language from the creature. When he told his tale to Victor, the creature also uses poetic language and linguistic devices such as the simile 'like lichen on a rock'. Because of the Russian doll narrative form that Shelley employs, the voice of the creature is furthest away from the reader and filtered through both Victor's and Walton's biased view of the creature because of his appearance. This means that the reader never gets to hear the voice of the creature directly; the fact that he still talks with such eloquence despite the bias of Victor and Walton means that the reader is further convinced of his inherent good nature, thereby sympathising with the creature.

Shelley also directs the reader's sympathy by using words from the lexical field of religion. The juxtaposition of negative religious words ('flames' and 'blasted' to describe the creature's existence on earth and the living world) with positive religious words ('ascend' and 'peace' to describe dying) highlights his unjust treatment and how 'miserable' his existence on earth has been, thus eliciting pathos in the reader. Likewise, the anaphora of the phrase 'I shall' shows the creature accepting his death. He becomes a martyr-like figure through his reference to a 'funeral pile' and 'torturing flames', which redeems him in the eyes of the reader. This is also presented as a contrast to Victor, who is described in the rest of the novel as not respecting the dead, dabbling in 'unhallowed arts' and 'playing' God, something that would have alienated Shelley's original readers in particular.

In conclusion, by ending with the creature telling his side of the story before his death, Shelley leaves the reader with sympathies for the creature rather than Victor. Throughout the novel, Shelley criticises Victor for experimenting with unnatural ideas and being the cause of his own demise through failing to be a proper parent towards the creature. In this final passage, Victor is not mentioned at all, suggesting that, despite the title, this is in fact the story of the creature rather than his creator. Therefore, the closing impression for the reader is that of sympathy towards the creature.

What an amazing answer! As you can see, a detailed knowledge of your set text is essential. You might not remember dozens of quotations, but must at least be able to refer to these moments.

Buy 'Mr Bruff's Guide to 'Frankenstein'' at www.mrbruff.com

Now let's explore another response that is adapted from a contribution from student Aaron Brooks. In his answer, he has a roughly 50:50 split between a close analysis of the extract and a discussion of how the theme of the supernatural relates to the rest of the novella.

Example Response for Section B: Charles Dickens's 'A Christmas Carol'

Explore how Dickens presents the supernatural:

a) In this extract
b) In the novel as a whole

[30 marks]

It was a strange figure—like a child: yet not so like a child as like an old man, viewed through some supernatural medium, which gave him the appearance of having receded from the view, and being diminished to a child's proportions. Its hair, which hung about its neck and down its back, was white as if with age; and yet the face had not a wrinkle in it, and the tenderest bloom was on the skin. The arms were very long and muscular; the hands the same, as if its hold were of uncommon strength. Its legs and feet, most delicately formed, were, like those upper members, bare. It wore a tunic of the purest white and round its waist was bound a lustrous belt, the sheen of which was beautiful. It held a branch of fresh green holly in its hand; and, in singular contradiction of that wintry emblem, had its dress trimmed with summer flowers. But the strangest thing about it was, that from the crown of its head there sprung a bright clear jet of light, by which all this was visible; and which was doubtless the occasion of its using, in its duller moments, a great extinguisher for a cap, which it now held under its arm.

Even this, though, when Scrooge looked at it with increasing steadiness, was not its strangest quality. For as its belt sparkled and glittered now in one part and now in another, and what was light one instant, at another time was dark, so the figure itself fluctuated in its distinctness: being now a thing with one arm, now with one leg, now with twenty legs, now a pair of legs without a head, now a head without a body: of which dissolving parts, no outline would be visible in the dense gloom wherein they melted away. And in the very wonder of this, it would be itself again; distinct and clear as ever.

"Are you the Spirit, sir, whose coming was foretold to me?" asked Scrooge.

"I am!"

The voice was soft and gentle. Singularly low, as if instead of being so close beside him, it were at a distance.

"Who, and what are you?" Scrooge demanded.

"I am the Ghost of Christmas Past."

"Long past?" inquired Scrooge: observant of its dwarfish stature.

"No. Your past."

Perhaps, Scrooge could not have told anybody why, if anybody could have asked him; but he had a special desire to see the Spirit in his cap; and begged him to be covered.

"What!" exclaimed the Ghost, "would you so soon put out, with worldly hands, the light I give? Is it not enough that you are one of those whose passions made this cap, and force me through whole trains of years to wear it low upon my brow!"

Scrooge reverently disclaimed all intention to offend or any knowledge of having wilfully bonneted the Spirit at any period of his life. He then made bold to inquire what business brought him there.

Your welfare!" said the Ghost.

Scrooge expressed himself much obliged, but could not help thinking that a night of unbroken rest would have been more conducive to that end. The Spirit must have heard him thinking, for it said immediately:

"Your reclamation, then. Take heed!"

EXAMPLE ANSWER

The supernatural is used by Dickens as an allegory for necessary change in the upper strata of Victorian society. The supernatural Ghosts who visit the protagonist Scrooge serve to guide him towards becoming a better person. This is a moral message to contemporary readers who, like readers today, are encouraged to reflect upon their attitudes to the poor and their own role in society.

With the first Ghost, the Ghost of Christmas Past, Dickens uses colour to present the ghost as a symbol of goodness: it wears 'a tunic of the purest white'. The superlative adjective 'purest' followed by the adjective 'white' symbolise innocence and connote kindness. Therefore, Dickens presents the Ghost as a benign creature, there to help Scrooge. There is more symbolism with the Ghost's face, which has 'not a wrinkle in it'. This connotes youth, and contemporary Victorian literature presents children as innocent and angelic. Therefore, the description of a young face alludes to an idea of purity and goodness. This emphasises the innocence of childhood before we—and significantly Scrooge—make decisions that affect the future and change us as people. This might be a metaphor for the choices that the miserly rich make in society.

Dickens also uses light imagery to present the Ghost as a symbol of truth and enlightenment. The Ghost has a 'bright clear jet of light' coming from the crown of his head. Scrooge literally struggles to face the light. Metaphorically, this could be because the light is a symbol of truth and memory, which he is trying to avoid. The adjectives 'bright' and 'clear' suggest that there is a lot of truth to be learned by Scrooge. Furthermore, 'light' is traditionally associated with the ideas of purity, goodness and truth. Scrooge 'begged' the spirit to cover the light with his cap. This suggests that Scrooge is not ready to face the truth of the past. This could also be a metaphor for how the rich in Victorian society choose to turn a blind eye to the poverty that surrounds them. The symbol of light is further explored with the belt that 'sparkled and glittered' in different places, making the shape of the Ghost of Christmas Past difficult to pin down. The sparkle and glitter of the belt suggest that memories are always changing and being reshaped by experience. Scrooge will shortly have to re-examine his memories of the past. Perhaps this is Dickens's way of encouraging the reader to reflect on key moments in the reader's past.

Dickens employs direct speech to emphasise the Ghost's good intentions. When it speaks, it references the abstract nouns 'welfare' and 'reclamation'. These words have positive connotations; however, the fact that they are abstract nouns makes them intangible, not easy to grasp, just as Scrooge is at this point in the novella, far from his salvation.

The Ghost forms part of the rising action (Freytag's pyramid), and his function is to guide Scrooge back in time and remind him of his past. All the Ghosts in the novella encourage Scrooge to examine his life and to change. Dickens therefore uses the supernatural as a structural feature to encourage change in society.

Elsewhere in the novella, Dickens introduces the Ghost of Christmas Present in Stave Three with a long list of food: the Ghost sits upon 'turkeys, geese, game, poultry, brawn, great joints of meat, sucking-pigs, long wreaths of sausages… and seething bowls of punch'. Dickens uses the device of listing to create visual symbolism of the generosity of the Ghost. The quantity of food suggests there is enough food to go around; this contradicts the Malthusian economic theory that population growth will outpace the production of food. This is a theory that Dickens hated, and he is therefore making the point that we can afford to be generous, especially to the poor who need it most.

We also see the supernatural through the personification of Ignorance and Want, which hide under the cloak of the Ghost of Christmas Present. It is significant Dickens places them under the cloak of this particular Ghost, as Dickens seems to be saying that the effects of these 'two children' are with present day Victorian society and so cannot be avoided. Therefore, Dickens uses the supernatural to make a social comment on deprivation. The children are described as are 'yellow, meagre, ragged, scowling, wolfish'. The list of negative adjectives emphasises the effects of mistreatment and contrasts with the positive use of listing when we first met the Ghost of Christmas Present. The adjective 'yellow' is unhealthy, suggesting malnutrition. This might be a metaphor for the spiritual illness in Victorian society, an illness suffered by those who are ignorant about the needs to the poor. The Ghost tells Scrooge that 'Ignorance' is more harmful than 'Want'; this could be Dickens criticising the rich for ignoring the poor.

Finally, Dickens introduces the Ghost of Christmas Yet to Come. Dickens uses the ghost to remind Scrooge (and the reader) that we all must die, so we should think about our relationships with others and how we will be remembered. The third Ghost is described as a Grim Reaper archetype: it is 'shrouded in a deep black garnet, which concealed its head, its face, its form'. The adjective 'black' connotes death, which scares the reader. The concealed 'head', 'face' and 'form' make the Ghost more horrific, mysterious and terrifying. This is a direct contrast to the approachability of the other Ghosts. This would have been frightening to contemporary readers as well as to modern readers. Perhaps Dickens deliberately employs this description to encourage the reader to reflect upon how they live their lives.

The Ghost of Christmas Yet to Come also shows Scrooge, and by default the reader, the consequences of living a life without helping others. Scrooge is called 'Old Scratch', which a Victorian audience would have recognised as meaning the devil. Dickens makes an apparent social remark on how people like Scrooge are devilish in their actions. Other men make remarks about Scrooge, saying they are 'disinterested'. The adjective 'disinterested' suggests that if you do not help others, no one will care for you once you are dead. Scrooge has clearly failed to make an impression in society. Furthermore, the fact that people will only go to Scrooge's funeral if 'lunch is provided' demonstrates how food is more of a reason to go, rather than honouring Scrooge's memory.

The above response does an excellent job of linking its analysis to Victorian society and Dickens's purpose of writing.

Buy 'Mr Bruff's Guide to 'A Christmas Carol' at www.mrbruff.com

The Importance of Genre
Now let's explore genre in more detail. Genre links to context because it is a writing style characterised by particular elements that are popular at the time of writing.

Many of the texts in Section B are part of a specific genre (for example, the 'Frankenstein' analysis referenced the horror genre). Knowing about specific genres and their conventions can help you to understand and analyse a text.

Let's take a look at Arthur Conan Doyle's 'The Sign of Four' as an example.

GENRE: 'THE SIGN OF THE FOUR'
Just as with the horror, romance or science-fiction genres, detective fiction has its own conventions and devices that appear regularly throughout the novel. The Sherlock Holmes novels, some of the earliest detective stories, certainly helped to shape many of the literary structures we would identify as belonging to the detective fiction genre. Genre is closely linked to form, as is tells us more about what to expect in the content of the writing.

Edgar Allen Poe, writing in the 19th century, is widely credited as being the first proponent of detective fiction in the West. While historically, detective stories have existed in other cultures such as in China and the Arab world, the detective genre as we know it today stems from the early 19th century. Poe wrote 'The Murders in the Rue Morgue' (first published in a magazine in 1841) that was influenced by a short story by E.T.A. Hoffman, written in 1819. Poe's story presents for the first time many of the devices that we would recognise in Arthur Conan Doyle's stories—specifically the close friend as a narrator (Watson) and the devilishly crafted barriers to detection.

In 'The Murders in the Rue Morgue', a mother and daughter have been murdered in a fourth-floor room of a building on the Rue Morgue, a fictional street in Paris. The door is locked from the inside, the mother's throat is slashed, and the daughter is strangled and stuffed in the chimney. The case baffles the police so Dupin, the story's amateur detective, offers his assistance. He ultimately unravels the story and solves the mystery, much to the embarrassment of the local police chief.

In the Sherlock Holmes story, there is constant tension between Holmes, who engages in reason, science and logic, and the police, who are depicted as bumbling, brutish and clumsy. This gives Holmes an air of superiority over the police who, although being put out by his obvious superiority, are usually glad of his help by the end of the story. Holmes also displays his astonishing abilities in the field of deduction and reasoning, which are key characteristics of the detective genre.

Some of the most basic conventions of the genre in general are:

The detective must be intriguing for the reader
It's important that the detective appears an outsider to those involved with the case. This is often presented through strange quirks or mannerisms of the detective. Holmes in many of the stories displays many strange habits: rushing off, with unannounced disappearances; asking strange questions; and, of course, his party trick of being able to deduce the most remarkable facts about a person, simply by looking at them. Add to this Holmes's abhorrence for 'the dull routine of existence', his predilection for heroin and cocaine, and you have a consulting detective which, according to Holmes is a profession he 'created... for I am the only one in the world'.

The crime must be worthy of investigation
The crime to be investigated must be important enough to attract the attention of such an important detective. Most cases in the detective genre involve either murder or the theft of an incredibly valuable item. It also must be significant in terms of its background: a case that is simple to solve is of no interest to the detective. Holmes himself admits that he 'craves for mental exaltation' and, in 'The Sign of Four', he rubs his hands together and his 'eyes glisten' when he hears the outline of the case.

The facts must be presented to the reader at the same time as the detective
To keep the reader engaged, the facts of the case should be presented to the reader at the same time as to the detective. This gives the reader a chance to interpret the clues and solve the case before the detective can. There is almost a sense of competition between the reader and the detective as to who can solve the mystery first.
In the case of Sherlock Holmes, this only serves to underline his amazing abilities even further, as he utilises his powers of deduction and logic to solve a hitherto impenetrable puzzle.

All the loose ends must be tied up by the end of the story
All good detective stories wrap up the different plot strands by the end of the story but, most importantly, always in a logical and understandable way. The end of the story is the opportunity for the detective to explain just how he solved the case and put all the

clues together. The ending should make sense to the reader and further impress on him or her the skills of the detective in unlocking the mystery.

Just like section A, section B requires you to present a line of argument and to analyse language, structure and form. Let's look at an example response.

Example Response for Section B: Conan Doyle's 'The Sign of the Four'

Explore how Conan Doyle presents ideas to do with wealth:

a) In this extract
b) In the novel as a whole

[30 marks]

"What a pretty box!" she said, stooping over it. "This is Indian work, I suppose?"
"Yes; it is Benares metal-work."
"And so heavy!" she exclaimed, trying to raise it. "The box alone must be of some value. Where is the key?"
"Small threw it into the Thames," I answered. "I must borrow Mrs. Forrester's poker." There was in the front a thick and broad hasp, wrought in the image of a sitting Buddha. Under this I thrust the end of the poker and twisted it outward as a lever. The hasp sprang open with a loud snap. With trembling fingers I flung back the lid. We both stood gazing in astonishment. The box was empty!

No wonder that it was heavy. The iron-work was two-thirds of an inch thick all round. It was massive, well made, and solid, like a chest constructed to carry things of great price, but not one shred or crumb of metal or jewellery lay within it. It was absolutely and completely empty.

"The treasure is lost," said Miss Morstan, calmly.

As I listened to the words and realized what they meant, a great shadow seemed to pass from my soul. I did not know how this Agra treasure had weighed me down, until now that it was finally removed. It was selfish, no doubt, disloyal, wrong, but I could realize nothing save that the golden barrier was gone from between us. "Thank God!" I ejaculated from my very heart.

She looked at me with a quick, questioning smile. "Why do you say that?" she asked.

"Because you are within my reach again," I said, taking her hand. She did not withdraw it. "Because I love you, Mary, as truly as ever a man loved a woman. Because this treasure, these riches, sealed my lips. Now that they are gone I can tell you how I love you. That is why I said, 'Thank God.'"

"Then I say, 'Thank God,' too," she whispered, as I drew her to my side. Whoever had lost a treasure, I knew that night that I had gained one.

The answer on the next page is based on a submission by student Harry Wintle:

EXAMPLE ANSWER

This extract follows the climax of the story when Small and Tonga are chased down the River Thames. It is part of the falling action of the novel, recounted with Watson's narrative voice. This encourages the reader to focus on his thoughts and feelings about Mary Morstan in relation to the treasure chest and the impact of money on their relationship.

By learning that the chest is empty at the same time as Watson, the reader is experiencing a typical feature of the detective genre in that the puzzle is unravelled and solved at the same time for the reader as it is for the detective and in this case, Watson and Mary). This aspect of the literary context heightens the impact not only for Watson and Mary but also for the reader when Conan Doyle presents the theme of money through the relationship between the characters of Watson and Mary. Conan Doyle employs direct speech when Watson uses the exclamatory sentence 'Thank God' upon discovering the Agra treasure chest is empty. This adds shock as it is unexpected, et the reader, who has shares Watson's feelings about Mary throughout the novel understands that for Watson, although treasure is physical but it is also a metaphor for how we value those we love. This shows that for him, his love of Mary is the true treasure rather than the jewels. In the Victorian times, middle- and upper-class men we expected to support their wives financially; had Mary been a rich woman, her status would have risen, and society would have frowned upon her marrying Watson, who would be poorer than her. Watson is well aware of this, so paradoxically, the Agra chest represents something that stands in the way of gaining the treasure of Mary's love.

Conan also presents parallel ideas about wealth being a burden, and this helps the reader to understand the relationship between Watson and Mary. Watson uses the metaphor the 'Agra treasure weighed me down'. This shows that for character of Watson the treasure, something that is supposed to bring riches and happiness, only brings sorrow. This is also seen with Mary's manner of speaking: she says that the treasure is lost and Conan Doyle uses the adverb 'calmly'. Why would Conan use this adverb when she just lost the chance of becoming the richest woman in London? Because the treasure is a curse, not a gift, and the curse is lifted when the treasure is gone. This makes the reader realise the double, and sometimes contrasting, effects that some objects hold. It also reveals a parallel response from Watson and Mary, which in itself might be symbolic of their compatibility.

Despite the treasure being a burden and an obstacle to their happiness, we have irony with the treasure used as a plot device to bring the characters of Mary and Watson together. This is part of the detective genre in which the whole purpose is to solve clues and uncover a crime. We see how the couple comes together at the end of the extract when Watson 'drew her to my side.' This active sentence with Watson being the subject and Mary the object symbolises the traditional active male role and the passive female role in Victorian society. This might represent how the status quo is now restored because Watson who no longer feed threatened by Mary's wealth is now able to show his love. Interestingly, Watson draws Mary to his 'side' and this symbolises that they will face the world together, foreshadowing their marriage.

Elsewhere in the novel, Conan Doyle also shows that treasure can be beautiful and the riches it brings can be amazing. This is shown then Small lays eyes on the treasure for the first time and sees 'glittering rubies, sapphires and emeralds'. The adjective 'glittering' emphasises the rule of three with the three nouns. This shows how attractive and tempting the gemstones are, as they are objects of beauty and fascination. Conan also makes the prospect of wealth more interesting by the fact that everyone is after the treasure, showing that everyone, no matter what their background, loves the idea of wealth. This makes the reader realise the literal beauty of treasure and how the idea of treasure is beautiful.

Conan Doyle also uses the theme of wealth to illustrate the deadly sin of greed and how it can bring out the worst in people. When he recounts the story of stealing the Agra treasure, Small initially has a conscience about killing the man who was transporting it to Agra, but he later helped to kill the Sikh 'in cold blood'; Tonga kills Sholto; and Small, when interrogated, says he said that he 'would have thought no more of knifing' the old major 'than of smoking this cigar '. This shows that although at first glance, treasure appears to be attractive, it can turn people into murderers. Perhaps this is a cautionary warning from Conan Doyle about the temptation of riches.

Harry has a clear thread of discussion throughout, as each paragraph deals with a different aspect of the impact of wealth or treasure on people's lives.

Buy 'Mr Bruff's Guide to 'The Sign of Four'' at mrbruff.com

Example Response for Section B: Charlotte Brontë's 'Jane Eyre'

GENRES
Unlike 'The Sign of the Four', Charlotte Brontë's 'Jane Eyre' combines three genres:

1. Bildungsroman

'Bildungsroman' is a German word that translates as 'education' ('Bildung') and novel ('Roman'). A Bildungsroman is therefore a novel about the growth of a central character through several periods of life. During 'Jane Eyre', we learn of Jane's internal and external conflicts in each new geographical setting. We can track her development by how she manages these conflicts.

When we first meet Jane at Gateshead, she is an outsider because of her status as a penniless orphan and dependent on her Aunt Reed. She is unable to control her passionate temper and rebels against her cousin and aunt. She has external conflicts with her family and internal ones when she thinks she can see her uncle's 'ghost' in the red-room. Under the influence of the positive female role models of Miss Temple and Helen Burns at Lowood School, Jane learns to control her passions.

Eight years later, she is working as a governess at Thornfield Hall where she falls in love with Mr Rochester. Jane's lower social status leads her to feel unworthy of Mr Rochester; with her plain appearance, she also feels inferior to 'the beautiful Blanche'. These internal self-doubts are paralleled by the external tensions surrounding the mysteries of the laughter; Grace Poole; Mr Mason after he has been attacked; and Bertha Rochester tearing Jane's wedding veil in half. Even when she agrees to marry Mr Rochester, she feels uncomfortable with him lavishing gifts on her, resulting in more internal conflict. Still further conflict is created when she learns that he is married, and she refuses his offer to become his mistress.

In the Moor House chapters, Jane suffers internal and external conflict when she becomes a beggar. As a school mistress, she subsequently has concerns about dropping in social rank. At the end of the Moor House chapters, a huge amount of emotional and spiritual conflict is created by St. John with his marriage proposals and cold ways. Jane almost rejects her own passions and accepts his proposal, but her supernatural connection with Mr Rochester makes her realise that she must marry for love. We have emotional conflict when she learns that Rochester Hall has burnt down and she does not know if Mr Rochester is still living. Finally, we have the famous line 'Reader, I married him', which shows that Jane actively makes choices and has become, for the time being at least, the dominant partner in the relationship.

Brontë challenges the tradition of gender hierarchy by writing from the point of view of a woman. This, combined with her beliefs about how women are restricted in Victorian society, emphasises that, in her view, a woman's inner development is of equal importance to a man's.

2. Romance

The novel's popularity when it was published was largely due to its style of writing; it was unusual for a novel to be written from a first-person female perspective, especially one that describes the narrator's feelings with such intensity. Moreover, at that time, the readership of novels was predominantly female, so Brontë's fans would better empathise with the thoughts and feelings of a female protagonist.

Jane's love interest Mr Rochester is not, like Jane, conventionally good-looking. However, with his 'dark face, stern features and heavy brow', he resembles a Byronic hero, a type of character, named after the English Romantic poet Lord Byron. A Byronic hero is a flawed hero, who is dark, mysterious, moody, rebellious, arrogant, brooding and passionate. By depicting Mr Rochester as a Byronic hero, not only Jane, but also many of her readers would be attracted to him.

Typical characteristics of the romance genre are that two people fall in love with each other, there is an obstacle, they overcome the obstacle, and they live happily ever after. In 'Jane Eyre', the obstacle is Bertha Rochester; she dies in a fire, so Jane and Mr Rochester can now marry and live happily ever after.

3. The Gothic Novel

The gothic genre combines Romanticism with fiction and horror. In gothic literature, characters usually include a virtuous orphaned heroine (who faints a lot) and a murderous villain with terrifying eyes. Tales are set in the past, often in remote foreign castles or monasteries with secret subterranean passages. Expect to encounter a vampire, ghost or monster. The weather is often horrible, and there will be a lot of melodrama.

This genre was popular in the Romantic Movement but, by the 1840s, it began to decline due to an increasing appetite for more socially realistic novels (such as those of Anthony Trollope). Brontë's success was her ability to combine elements of realism with gothic melodrama. Her orphaned heroine, for example, does not faint at the sight of blood.

EXAMPLE QUESTION

Explore how Brontë uses setting to develop atmosphere:
a) In this extract
b) And elsewhere in the novel

[30 marks]

A breakfast-room adjoined the drawing-room, I slipped in there. It contained a bookcase: I soon possessed myself of a volume, taking care that it should be one stored with pictures. I mounted into the window-seat: gathering up my feet, I sat cross-legged, like a Turk; and, having drawn the red moreen curtain nearly close, I was shrined in double retirement.

Folds of scarlet drapery shut in my view to the right hand; to the left were the clear panes of glass, protecting, but not separating me from the drear November day. At intervals, while turning over the leaves of my book, I studied the aspect of that winter afternoon. Afar, it offered a pale blank of mist and cloud; near a scene of wet lawn and storm-beat shrub, with ceaseless rain sweeping away wildly before a long and lamentable blast.

EXAMPLE ANSWER

This extract is from beginning of the novel. It is the exposition (Freytag's pyramid) in which we learn about Jane's character and the importance of setting. The setting creates a feeling of loneliness in the first paragraph with the repetition of the pronoun 'I', which is used five times to emphasise that Jane is in a separate room to the Reed family. However, Brontë's of choice of nouns implies Jane's self-reliance: 'bookcase' – 'volume' – 'pictures' – 'window-seat' and 'retirement' imply that she can adapt to her environment by finding solace in books. The simile 'like a Turk' provides evidence of her education (as does the fact that she knows the name of the material 'moreen') and that she is using her imagination as a coping strategy.

In the second paragraph, the setting contains vivid visual imagery of the 'red' or 'scarlet' of the curtains, which are strong gothic colours. These juxtapose with the pale colours outside the room to develop atmosphere. The colour red usually signifies blood or danger, which reminds us that the Reed home is not a comfortable place for her.

Another interpretation is that the 'scarlet drapery' is comforting womb-like imagery, which suggests that, like an unborn baby, Jane has not yet entered the world and is perhaps reluctant to do so. The pathetic fallacy and colourless imagery of the 'pale blank of mist and cloud' contrasts with the 'scarlet' and suggests a clash between Jane and her environment. She cannot at this stage see a way out of her situation, just as it is not possible to see through mist. The narrative structure unravels to reveal violent weather imagery at the end of the second paragraph. The imagery of the 'storm-beat shrub, with ceaseless rain' and the use of the onomatopoeia 'blast' combine to symbolise that Jane is vulnerable and at the mercy of her family. This imagery foreshadows aunt's abuse of her when she locks Jane in the 'red-room', providing more evidence of the unsettling atmosphere in the house.

This womb imagery contrasts with the horror of the 'red-room' at the end of the chapter when Jane is isolated and surrounded by the colour 'red'. The gothic use of red becomes hellish and, like a gothic heroine, Jane faints because of the overwhelming horror of seeing the ghostly light. Narrated in the first person, the older Jane reflects on her life as a child and guides the reader's response. This is important for later in the novel where we see a completely different reaction to her setting. For example, Mr Rochester asks Jane if she turns 'sick at the sight of blood' in chapter 20 because a contemporary stereotype was that women were so fragile and emotional that they would faint at the sight of blood. By helping Mr Rochester and not fainting, we can measure how Jane, who does not faint, is taking an active male role and mastering her response to a challenging setting by staunching Mr Mason's blood. This contrasts with her stereotypically passive female response of earlier fainting in the red-room, which is the colour of blood. Through Jane's responses to her setting, we therefore have a yardstick by which to measure her development, and Brontë challenges contemporary beliefs about women being weak.

Elsewhere in the novel, we see the influences of the gothic genre with the atmospheric setting of Jane's journey to Thornfield Hall through the 'misty' night. She hears the 'tolling' bell as they pass the church, and the entrance gates of Thornfield Hall 'clash' behind them. The 'dark' building is lit by 'candlelight'. These atmospheric words foreshadow elements of Jane's life. Like the mist outside the breakfast-room window at Gateshead, the mist on the journey to Thornfield Hall foreshadows Jane's future inability to see her situation clearly, as secrets will be hidden from her; bells usually toll at funerals, so the 'tolling' church bell could foreshadow the death of her hopes and expectations as well as the later death of Bertha Rochester; the 'clash' of the gates behind her might symbolise Bertha's imprisonment and Jane's future concerns about losing her identity in marriage; the 'dark' building could represent hidden secrets; and 'candlelight' has associations with Bertha's future attempts to burn down Thornfield, but might also remind the reader that, at Thornfield, Jane's passion and love for Mr Rochester will burn brightly. The gothic imagery therefore introduces the setting, creates a sense of mystery and unease, and develops the idea of events being controlled by the supernatural.

Buy 'Mr Bruff's Guide to 'Jane Eyre'' at mrbruff.com. Also available in hardback on Amazon.

English Literature Paper 2: Modern Texts and Poetry

At 2 hours and 15 minutes, this exam is the longest of all. It contains three sections and is marked out of 96:

- Section A: Modern prose or drama (worth 34 marks, four of which are awarded for spelling, punctuation and grammar)
- Section B: Poetry (worth 30 marks)
- Section C: Unseen poetry (worth 32 marks)

You should spend around 45 minutes on each section.

A reminder that the assessment objectives for this paper are weighted as follows:

GCSE English Literature, Paper 2		
AO1	Read, understand and respond to texts. Students should be able to: • maintain a critical style and develop an informed personal response • use textual references, including quotations, to support and illustrate interpretations.	22.5%
AO2	Analyse the language, form and structure used by a writer to create meanings and effects, using relevant subject terminology where appropriate.	27.5%
AO3	Show understanding of the relationships between texts and the contexts in which they were written.	7.5%
AO4	Use a range of vocabulary and sentence structures for clarity, purpose and effect, with accurate spelling and punctuation.	2.5%
	Percentage of final GCSE:	60%

This table contains public sector information licensed under the Open Government Licence v3.0.

The greatest focus should once again be given to analysis of language, structure and form. In simple terms, this means that writing about context should be present but not overly focused upon. We have already fully explored these assessment objectives earlier in this guide, so let's look at the exam.

Paper 2, Section A: Modern Prose or Drama

Let's take a look at a typical section A question. You will answer one question based on one of the following texts:

'A Taste of Honey' by Shelagh Delaney

'Animal Farm' by George Orwell

'An Inspector Calls' by JB Priestley:

'Anita and Me' by Meera Syal

'Blood Brothers' by Willy Russell

'DNA' by Dennis Kelly

'Lord of the Flies' by William Golding

'Never Let Me Go' by Kazuo Ishiguro

'Pigeon English' by Stephen Kelman

'Telling Tales' (AQA exam board Anthology)

'The Curious Incident of the Dog in the Night-Time' by Simon Stephens

'The History Boys' by Alan Bennett

As it is one of the most commonly studied texts, I shall base my answers on JB Priestley's 'An Inspector Calls'. Each set text will contain two questions; you must choose one to answer.

An Inspector Calls
CONTEXT AND PURPOSE OF WRITING

Sometimes a writer will choose to set their text in a different historical period to the one in which they are writing. When this happens, we need to ask ourselves *why* they have done this. Let's explore this idea further through taking a look at JB Priestley's 'An Inspector Calls', which was written in 1945 but set in 1912. Before you read on, think about the significance of those two years.

In 1912, when the play is set, the world had not experienced World War I or World War II. The ruling classes saw no need for change: they were keen to stay in power. The Birlings, a wealthy family, represent others of a similar social status. They are heavily criticised by Priestley in the play (via the role of the Inspector), as they initially take no responsibility for their actions and the effect they have on others. Any audience at the time (from 1946 to the present day) is aware that a family such as the Birlings would soon hear about the sinking of the Titanic and would then have to endure two world wars.

Priestley, having witnessed two world wars that were fought to save society, questions what kind of society people were fighting to save. The very idea of 'society' suggests a group working together and looking out for one another; taking social responsibility is vital. Seeing characters before the wars may provide some hope to Priestley's audience who had been through a very difficult period. The attitude of the Birlings and the way they are so quick to dismiss any involvement with the unpleasant nature of Eva's suicide would no doubt speak to an audience at the time, who had lived through the result of such complacency and ignorance. An audience in the late 1940s would still have been deprived of many of the luxuries that the Birlings enjoy at the beginning of the play, as rationing continued into the 1950s. The wealthy Birlings can therefore be seen as materialistic and superficial.

Priestley may well have set his play in 1912 because it started a time of great change. In the period between the two dates, class and gender differences were not so pronounced. As a result, there was hope for a better future if young people could be educated and take responsibility for their actions and their treatment of others.

As with Paper 1, you need to analyse language, structure and form to achieve the highest marks. With a text like 'An Inspector Calls' there are only really one or two contextual points which run throughout the entire text: the author's views on social responsibility and his criticism of capitalism. You will probably find yourself writing about this in any answer.

In the same way, answers on William Golding's 'Lord of the Flies' will almost always lend themselves to points about the innate evil in humankind. Not all texts are like this: some have a range of contextual themes, so make sure you are aware of all of them.

Unlike in Paper 1, there are no extracts given for these questions. I suppose the exam board feel that they make up for this by giving you two questions to choose from. You should memorise key quotations where possible, using the same method presented with 'Pride and Prejudice' earlier in this guide.

You should aim to write your answer in PEE paragraphs too, also covered earlier.

EXAMPLE QUESTION

Explore the significance of the character of Sheila in 'An Inspector Calls'.

[30 marks] & A04 [4 marks]

This response is based on a contribution by student Katie Hale.

Sheila is a significant character in the play because she symbolises hope for Priestley's message of socialism. As a member of the younger generation, she is more open to listening to the views of others, and she is not as entrenched in her views as her capitalist parents Mr and Mrs Birling.

In order to appreciate the change in Sheila, the audience needs first to see how she is presented at the beginning of the play. When we meet Sheila in Act 1, she is described in the stage directions as a 'pretty girl'. This adjective and noun reflect contemporary attitudes in which women were judged by their appearances: her thoughts and opinions are less important than her looks. At the start of the play, she behaves like a 'pretty girl' when she says 'Now I really feel engaged'. This shows that she is superficial as she cares about material things. This contrasts with the change in her character later in the play when the audience realises that she is now a mature woman, who accepts responsibility and has her own views ('between us, we helped to kill her'). Her views about social responsibility are now far more important than a decorative engagement ring. When she refuses to take the ring back from Gerald, saying it is 'too soon', we again see her character develop into an independent modern young lady. Her beliefs about social responsibility are now important than the traditional expectations of marriage.

Secondly, her change in character is shown by her use of language. In Act 1, she uses the term of address 'mummy'; this is a rather childish word for a young woman to use, and you would not expect a woman who has just become engaged to use it. Later in the play when she regrets her role in the death of Eva Smith, Sheila's vocabulary changes, and she calls Mrs Birling 'mother'. This shows that she has matured and no longer views the world through the eyes of a child. Priestley also employs the hyphen in many of Sheila's lines to show that she speaks her thoughts as she thinks them in a stream of consciousness. At the beginning of the play, she exclaims over the ring 'Oh – Gerald – you've got it – is it the one you wanted me to have?' and she sounds like a child unable to control her emotions. We also see contemporary attitudes to women in that Gerald chooses the ring. Yet at the end of the play, Sheila speaks in a more purposeful way, challenging her parents, saying 'I tell you – whoever that Inspector was, it was anything but a joke'. The hyphen shows that she is pausing to emphasise her point. This hyphen use therefore shows the steady progression of her change in terms of Priestley's guidance to how the actress playing Sheila is expected to read the lines. This impacts the audience who interpret her character: the change in vocabulary and hyphen use show the development of Sheila's thought process when she concludes that she needs to learn from her mistakes and develop more social responsibility.

We also see Sheila's growing independence through the attitudes that others have to her and her response to them. Mrs Birling calls her a 'hysterical' and 'childish' and Gerald is taken aback when she confronts him at the beginning of Act 2—she speaks 'bitterly' (stage directions) when he does not understand her reasons for wanting to stay to watch him being interrogated. I think Priestly does this to show that people will always regard Sheila as emotional rather than intellectual and that, in society, women find it hard to change other people's attitudes towards them. I think the real turning point for her character is when she joins the Inspector in turning on her mother, saying 'You turned her away—yes, and you killed her'. Sheila is now voicing the Inspector's and by default (as the Inspector is the mouthpiece of Priestley) Priestley's views. Priestley is therefore agreeing with her assertive, confrontational attitude in which she challenges the views of others, pressuring them to accept responsibility for Eva's death (just as socialist 'cranks' at the time were challenging capitalist views in society). Young women like Sheila might not be respected for their views just yet, but they are no longer passive.

To conclude, Priestley conveys many powerful messages through the change in Sheila's character. Priestley wants to convey that the materialistic girl can develop into a young, independent socialist, challenging views on capitalism. As a member of the younger generation, she also symbolises how the role of young women was beginning to change in 1912. Her character therefore represents hope for the future.

This answer is a great example of avoiding one of the key pitfalls in literature exams: writing as if the characters are real. With a question on Sheila, it would be easy to write about Sheila and the kind of character she is. However, all characters are used by writers to convey themes, so you must make sure you write about the author (in this case Priestley) and how he uses the character to convey themes. It is more important to write about the author and their themes than the characters.

As a special bonus, let's look at another answer–this one analyses the character of Inspector Goole. It was written by two students, Jamie Handitye and Thomas Phillips.

As you read the answer, highlight the following:
1) Analysis of language, structure and form
2) Analysis of the writer's ideas and themes
3) Analysis of relevant contextual features

The theme of responsibility is one of the key ideas within Priestley's 'An Inspector Calls'. It is effectively conveyed through Priestley's use of language, structure and form in the presentation of Inspector Goole, who interrogates the Birling family; he tries to convince them to see the error of their ways so they can take responsibility for all their actions.

Priestley begins the theme of responsibility and judgement through the awaited entrance of the Inspector. In Act One, before the Inspector enters, the stage directions state that the lighting should change from 'pink and intimate' to 'brighter and harder'. The use of the comparatives 'brighter' and 'harder' create the image of an interrogation with a 'brighter' light exposing the whole family's 'sins'. This is evident when Inspector Goole enters and forces the family to accept responsibility for Eva's death—Eva drank disinfectant that 'burnt her inside out'. The gruesome imagery that comes from the emotive verb 'burnt' shocks the Birling family; this contrasts from the nonchalant idiom 'inside out'. The juxtaposition between these two ideas is purposefully used by Priestley to emphasise the grave nature of this incident, evoking a sense of pathos from the audience towards Eva because they know these events happened as a result of the Birling family's actions. Cleverly here, Priestley draws the audience back to social responsibility and the lack of it within this household. Alternatively, Priestley might have been showing that the Birling family will never learn and it will only be 'harder' to redeem from their myopic view.

Priestly continues to convey this theme through the play through Goole's impactful messages. Before he exits, the Inspector asserts that 'We don't live alone. We are members of one body. We are responsible for each other'. The anaphora with the repetition of the pronoun 'we' emphasises the much-needed care for one another and also preaches the socialist ideal of the community over the individual. The united 'body' imagery suggests that pain is transferred throughout the body of humanity by mistreating others. This links to how Sybil Birling effectively kills her own grandchild and further reinforces the extremely important theme of responsibility.

Priestley employs religious imagery within Inspector Goole's warning that there will be 'fire and blood and anguish' if the lesson is not learnt from the death of Eva, a symbol of the proletariat. The polysyndetic list with its continuous use of the co-ordinating conjunction 'and' creates the impression that the Birlings will forever suffer if they do not take responsibility for their actions. This is reinforced by the noun 'fire', which has direct connotations of damnation and hell, instilling fear in the audience. Moreover, the 'blood' and 'anguish' might be hinting at a social revolution where the poor stand up against the ruling class, causing further divide and 'blood'. This aims to make the Birlings realise how important it is for them to be responsible for everyone else because they are the affluent people of that town. Finally, the list also foreshadows WW2 where class conflict would need to be put aside to fight Adolf Hitler: accepting responsibilities now would ensure protection.

In conclusion, through the speech and character of Inspector Goole, Priestley shows the need for social responsibility within this capitalist household that has been indoctrinated into a self-serving lifestyle.

You can buy 'Mr Bruff's Guide to 'An Inspector Calls" at www.mrbruff.com

Paper 2, Section B: Anthology Poetry

This section of the exam will require you to compare two poems. In class, you will study fifteen poems taken from one of two clusters: Power and Conflict or Love and Relationships. The named poem will be printed on the exam paper, along with a question. You must choose a second poem to compare—to help to jog your memory, the titles of all the poems in the cluster that you have studied will be listed on the exam paper.

The first thing you need to do in the exam is find the question that focuses on the cluster you've studied in class. Some students wonder if it's worth studying both clusters but, as each is made up of 15 poems, it would be too much to attempt to learn 30 poems (particularly as you need to memorise quotations). In this section, I will give detailed examples from both the Power and Conflict and cluster and the Love and Relationships cluster.

Hitting the Top Marks

This question is marked out of 30, and marking is divided into 6 bands. There are four major differences between band 5 and 6. Band 6 answers need to:

1. Analyse language, structure and form. Band 5 and below requires only one of these to be focused on, but band 6 demands consideration of all three areas.
2. Give an exploratory answer
3. Give precise references
4. Explore context.

By far the biggest challenge with these criteria is to analyse language **and** structure **and** form.

Language refers to the words that are used by the poet. A reminder that this is the simplest type of analysis and the one which most students write about first. Look for interesting words and phrases or poetic devices such as similes, alliteration, metaphors, personification and onomatopoeia.

Structure refers to the organisation of a poem—essentially, it means *how the poem is organised, and why this is significant.* Analysis of structure should consider the number of verses, where the verses change and why, variations in verse length, line length, use of enjambment, repetition, rhythm, changes in stress patterns, use of rhyme scheme, free verse and punctuation. However, it's not just a case of identifying these features. They need to be linked to the theme of the poem. So, we only want to analyse that exclamation mark at the end of the poem if we can somehow link it to the exam question that you are answering.

Form refers to the times when poets follow particular rules about the organisation of a text. For example, is the poem a sonnet, a haiku, a limerick, a dramatic monologue, a ballad, etc.? All of these forms have specific conventions. Does the poem follow them fully?

My biggest piece of advice for hitting the top grades is to analyse structure and form wherever possible. Have them at the forefront of your mind. Look for structure and form first, and write about them first in the exam. The top marks in the poetry exam are given to those students who stand out from the rest. If 90% of students are analysing language for most of their answers, you can be different.

How to Analyse Poetry: Power and Conflict

Many students find analysing a poem very confusing. Let's take a detailed look through two poems from the Power and Conflict cluster: 'My Last Duchess' and 'Ozymandias'. Then we will look at an example answer to an exam question.

ROBERT BROWNING'S 'MY LAST DUCHESS'

The Poet

When analysing any poem, it is important to only study those biographical details of the poet's life that seem key to understanding the poem itself. With 'My Last Duchess' this poses quite a challenge: Browning's dramatic monologue is not written from his own point of view but that of a fictional character. 'My Last Duchess' is set in the Italian Renaissance and focuses on a possibly insane Duke, who has full control. How can that possibly link to the poet's own life?

Nevertheless, there are some biographical details worth looking at which might help us understand the poem a little better:

1. Browning was born in 1812 in London. He died in 1889 in Venice.

2. Browning didn't enjoy school much and ended up being home-schooled by tutors, who educated him using his father's collection of 6,000 books. This brave move paid off: by the age of fourteen, he was fluent in Latin, Greek, French and Italian. Aged twelve, Robert wrote his first book of poetry.

3. In 1838, Browning visited Italy for the first time. He would live there for much of his adult life. In his poem 'De Gustibus', he wrote 'open my heart and you will see graved inside of it, Italy'.

4. 'My Last Duchess' was published in 1842.

5. In 1845, Browning married Elizabeth Barrett. Barrett is a famous poet in her own right. However, the marriage was kept secret to begin with, as Elizabeth's father was domineering and controlling.

What can we conclude from these details? Well, firstly we can see that the poet lived during the Victorian era. I will look at the importance of this in a moment.

Secondly, the details of Barrett's controlling attitude towards his daughter pose a striking resemblance to the Duke in 'My Last Duchess'. However, this is a red herring: Browning did not meet Elizabeth Barrett until 1846, four years after the publication of the poem. As much as it might seem a nice comparison, the character of the Duke is clearly not based on Browning's father-in-law.

The fact that Browning visited Italy shortly before the publication of the poem would suggest that it might be based on a story he heard whilst travelling (more on that later).

The Context

A reminder that the term 'context' essentially means what was happening at the time the poem was written. Although 'My Last Duchess' is set in the Italian Renaissance (14th - 16th century), it was written and published during the Victorian era in 1842. We should therefore examine the Victorian era to see if there is anything that seems important to our understanding of the poem.

One of the major issues with studying context is that it can take hundreds of hours of study, much of which might revolve around topics that are irrelevant to the poem being studied. My advice is to look at the general contextual topics and think carefully about which you should study further.

When 'My Last Duchess' was published in 1842, this was the early part of the Victorian era. During this period, there were many changes:

1. Industrialisation saw mass migration from the country to the city. In 1837, 80% of the population lived in the countryside. Most people worked on farms or spun wool, etc. With the Industrial Revolution came machines that could complete this work in a fraction of the time. As a result, people began moving to the cities to get work and, within a dozen or so years, 50% of the population lived in the city.

2. Romanticism: the poem was written in the Romantic literary movement (1798 - 1870). As a reaction to the changes in Britain through the Industrial Revolution, many Romantics glorified nature. When reading literature from this period, there are often idyllic descriptions of mountains, nature and the countryside. We see the

Romantic influence of the Duchess being pleased with the gift of a 'bough of cherries' and her appreciation of the 'dropping of the daylight'.

3. Attitudes to religion were being challenged due to the theory of evolution and scientific developments that seemingly disproved some Biblical passages. There are some minor ways in which religion can be linked to the poem, but these can be understood mostly in terms of the treatment of women, which is a topic in its own right.

4. Attitudes to women were changing. In 1792, Mary Wollstonecraft (mother of Mary Shelley, author of 'Frankenstein' published 'A Vindication of the Rights of Woman', which argued that women should receive the same education as men. 'My Last Duchess' was published in 1842 and in 1854, Coventry Patmore wrote a poem about his wife entitled 'The Angel in the House', in which she was described as a model for all women—gracious, submissive and self-sacrificing. This poem became very popular and influential because the whole point of her existence was to serve and entertain her husband. Although the idea of the woman's role as the 'angel of the house' emerged after the publication of 'My Last Duchess', it reflects contemporary attitudes to women against a backdrop of controversy about women's education and rights.

Here are a few brief notes about the treatment of English women in the 1800s:

- When a woman married, she became the legal property of her husband
- Women could not testify in court
- Women could not vote
- It was believed that women were incapable of rational thought
- Many female writers published their works anonymously or under male pseudonyms to boost book sales and to be taken seriously. Jane Austen, the Brontë sisters and Mary Ann Evans, better known as George Eliot, published their novels in this way.

This theme of attitudes to women seems to be the main contextual factor in the poem, as the whole poem explores attitudes to the duchess. Could it be that Browning uses the poem to explore his opinion on this topic? I think so!

It is possible to see the poem as a criticism of Victorian attitudes to women and the effort of men to suppress female sexuality. It can be argued that the duke's obsession with controlling the behaviour of his wife links to Victorian society's obsession with the idea of a perfect woman.

A feminist interpretation of the poem would suggest that Victorian men were weakened by their dependency on the power they had over women. The way in which Victorian men might have been obsessed with their power over women certainly links with the poem. Men in Victorian England saw their wives as a reflection of themselves.

The Italian Connection

The historical basis of the poem has been speculated about since it was first published. There are many ideas about the poem but nothing which is known for sure other than the following details:

1. Many of Browning's poems, including 'My Last Duchess', are set in Ferrara, a town in Italy. Browning seems obsessed with the place, researching the medieval history of the area. It seems likely that 'My Last Duchess' is based on the true story of Alfonso II, fifth Duke of Ferrara. Alfonso's first wife died in suspicious circumstances and many thought that he had poisoned her, so there is a strong case for the poem being based on this duke. However, this kind of detail should only be mentioned in an exam if it is relevant to a point about the poem's use of language, structure or form.
2. Browning is not the first poet to focus his work on the lives of despotic Italians. Dante's 'Inferno' recounts a number of stories of various cruel Italians. John Keats is another poet who focuses on a similar topic in his poem 'Isabella'.

The Literal Meaning

Once we understand important details about the poet and the context, we should look at the poem itself. All poems that are studied for exams have a simple literal meaning and at least one hidden deeper meaning. Our starting point should be to make sure we understand the basic meaning of the poem. It's a useful exercise to translate the poem into simple, understandable English. Where a line is ambiguous or has different meanings, begin by thinking of the simplest meaning. Here is my translation of the poem with the original version next to it:

Original	Translation
That's my last Duchess painted on the wall, Looking as if she were alive. I call That piece a wonder, now; Fra Pandolf's hands Worked busily a day, and there she stands.	That's a painting of my last wife on the wall. It looks as if she is still alive. I would say that the painting is a very realistic portrait. A famous artist worked hard for days painting it, and there she is.
Will't please you sit and look at her? I said "Fra Pandolf" by design, for never read Strangers like you that pictured countenance, The depth and passion of its earnest glance, But to myself they turned (since none puts by The curtain I have drawn for you, but I) And seemed as they would ask me, if they durst,	Will you please sit down and look at the painting? I name-dropped the famous artist on purpose, because people never look at it without wanting to ask me how the passionate look on her face was arrived at. They always ask me this question because I am the only one who pulls back the curtain that covers the painting. You are not the first person to ask (how the look was arrived at).

How such a glance came there; so, not
the first
Are you to turn and ask thus. Sir, 'twas
not
Her husband's presence only, called that
spot
Of joy into the Duchess' cheek; perhaps
Fra Pandolf chanced to say, "Her mantle
laps
Over my lady's wrist too much," or "Paint
Must never hope to reproduce the faint
Half-flush that dies along her throat."
Such stuff
Was courtesy, she thought, and cause
enough
For calling up that spot of joy. She had
A heart—how shall I say?— too soon
made glad,
Too easily impressed; she liked whate'er
She looked on, and her looks went
everywhere.
Sir, 'twas all one! My favour at her breast,
The dropping of the daylight in the West,
The bough of cherries some officious fool
Broke in the orchard for her, the white
mule
She rode with round the terrace—all and
each
Would draw from her alike the approving
speech,
Or blush, at least. She thanked men—
good! but thanked
Somehow—I know not how—as if she
ranked
My gift of a nine-hundred-years-old name
With anybody's gift. Who'd stoop to
blame
This sort of trifling? Even had you skill
In speech—which I have not—to make
your will
Quite clear to such an one, and say, "Just
this
Or that in you disgusts me; here you
miss,
Or there exceed the mark"—and if she let
Herself be lessoned so, nor plainly set

No, it was not only me (her husband) who
could make her look so happy. It might be
that the artist flattered her in some way,
perhaps saying that her shawl was too
long (and should be pulled up a bit). Or
maybe he told her it would be impossible
for paint to reproduce such a beautiful
woman. She was delighted to hear this
and blushed.

She was a woman who was too easily
impressed by things. She liked everything
she looked at, and she looked at
everything. It was all the same–the effect
I had on her was the same effect as the
sunset, or some cherries an admirer
brought to her, or her white mule–
everything impressed her and made her
happy, blushing with delight.

She thanked people, which was good, but
she thanked people in such a way that it
made me feel as if she wasn't sufficiently
grateful for the ancient and honoured
surname which became hers when we
married. Who would lower themselves to
argue with her? Even if I were a good
enough communicator to do it (and I am
not), I would not do it. It would mean that I
would have to lower myself, and I never
lower myself to tell her that 'this or that in
you disgusts me', or 'here you are going
too far', etc.

Her wits to yours, forsooth, and made excuse—
E'en then would be some stooping; and I choose
Never to stoop. Oh, sir, she smiled, no doubt,
Whene'er I passed her; but who passed without
Much the same smile? This grew; I gave commands;
Then all smiles stopped together. There she stands
As if alive. Will't please you rise? We'll meet
The company below, then. I repeat,
The Count your master's known munificence
Is ample warrant that no just pretense
Of mine for dowry will be disallowed;
Though his fair daughter's self, as I avowed
At starting, is my object. Nay, we'll go
Together down, sir. Notice Neptune, though,
Taming a sea-horse, thought a rarity,
Which Claus of Innsbruck cast in bronze for me!

Oh, sir, she smiled whenever I passed her, but she gave the same smile to everyone! This continued, and I gave commands. Then there were no more smiles. But in this painting, she looks alive.

Will you please stand up? We'll meet the others downstairs. I repeat, the Count, your master, is so rich that I'm sure he will give me a nice financial incentive to marry his daughter. But what I want is the daughter, not the money. See this statue? It's of Neptune, taming a sea-horse. It's a rare statue by another famous artist.

Themes

Now we understand the basics of the poem, it's important to consider the major themes: what is this poem trying to say? We need to move beyond what happens in the poem (the subject) to what the poem is trying to say (its theme).

'My Last Duchess' has a number of themes, but all of them revolve around one major one: power.

There are many types of power demonstrated in the poem:

> **a. Political power.** The duke's political power is demonstrated through the ambiguous line 'I gave commands'. The reader is left wondering who these commands were given to—no doubt a social inferior or servant of some kind.

> **b. Domestic power**. The Duke asserts his power over his former wife, linking to themes of gender roles and sexism.

Language, Structure and Form

Now we have the major theme defined, we shall look at how the poem explores that theme through the three poetic study areas of language, structure and form:

Language

Let's begin by establishing whether or not the duke had any cause for concern with his last wife. When the duke explains that 'her looks went everywhere', the reader is left wondering if he is implying that his wife was promiscuous. However, the doubts he has about the artist (more on that in a moment) should help the reader to decide that this was not the case.

It is clear that the duke was disgusted with his previous wife, the duchess. However, it is ironic to note that the duchess's faults were actually to exhibit qualities such as humility and gratitude. It seems the duchess was pleased by the simple things in life such as 'the dropping of the daylight'. In fact, she seems to have a childlike innocence to her, but this is not as positive as it may seem. The 19th-century feminist writer Mary Wollstonecraft once wrote that while 'children…should be innocent…when the epithet is applied to men, or women, it is but a civil term for weakness'. In other words, the wife is presented by the duke as weak and undeserving of such an amazing husband!

No, it seems that the duke had no valid reason to dislike his last wife, and so we must examine his character further to discover just what kind of man he is. Let's take a closer look at the characterisation of the duke, annotating significant language points.

> My Last Duchess
> That's <u>my</u> last Duchess painted on the wall,

The pronoun 'my' is repeated throughout the poem, showing how **possessive** the duke is. It also highlights how he objectifies women.

> Looking as if she were alive. I call
> That piece a wonder, now: <u>Frà Pandolf's</u> hands

The duke namedrops two famous artists, Fra Pandolf and Claus of Innsbruck, demonstrating that he is a **vain** person and that he is wealthy.

> Worked busily a day, and there she stands.
> Will 't please you sit and look at her? I said
> '<u>Frà</u> Pandolf' by design, for never read

The title 'Fra' means 'brother' (as in a religious figure). The suggestion here is that the portrait was painted by a monk or similar religious figure. Why is this important? Well, it seems that Browning wants to make it clear that the artist was not at all sexually involved in the duchess. There is no possibility that they were flirting or even having an affair, which makes it clearer that the Duke had no reason to be so jealous of his wife.

> Strangers like you that pictured countenance,
> The depth and passion of its earnest glance,

But to myself they turned (since none puts by
The curtain I have drawn for you, but I)
And seemed as they would ask me, if they durst,
How such a glance came there; so, not the first
Are you to turn and ask thus. <u>Sir</u>, 't was not

Browning uses language to highlight issues of power in the poem. The manner in which the duke speaks to the envoy is through the terms 'sir' and 'you'. These are formal terms of address that clarify the duke's superiority over the envoy. The more personal terms of 'thou' and 'thee' are not used. The duke is keen to point out that the envoy is socially inferior to him. This behaviour is **condescending**.

Her husband's presence only, called that spot
Of joy into the Duchess' cheek: perhaps
Frà Pandolf chanced to say, 'Her mantle laps
Over my lady's wrist too much,' or 'Paint
Must never hope to reproduce the faint
Half-flush that dies along her throat:' such stuff
Was courtesy, she thought, and cause enough
For calling up that spot of joy. She had
A heart -- how shall I say? -- too soon made glad,
Too easily impressed; she liked whate'er
She looked on, and her looks went everywhere.
Sir, 't was all one! My favour at her breast,
The dropping of the daylight in the West,
The bough of cherries some officious fool
Broke in the orchard for her, the white mule
She rode with round the terrace -- all and each
Would draw from her alike the approving speech,
Or blush, at least. She thanked men, -- good! but thanked
Somehow -- I know not how -- as if she ranked
<u>*My gift of a nine-hundred-years-old name*</u>

The duke is **proud**, feeling that his wife should be grateful to join in his family heritage and take his surname, which is so ancient and esteemed.

With anybody's gift. Who'd stoop to blame
This sort of trifling? Even had you skill
In speech -- (<u>which I have not</u>) -- to make your will

The duke is **disingenuous** in this moment. He tells the envoy that he does not possess skill in speaking whilst at the time using perfect iambic pentameter.

Quite clear to such an one, and say, 'Just this
Or that in you disgusts me; here you miss,
Or there exceed the mark' -- and if she let
Herself be lessoned so, nor plainly set

Her wits to yours, forsooth, and made excuse,
-- E'en then would be some stooping; and I choose

The duke is **self-obsessed**, seen through the repetition of the pronoun 'I'--it's all about him!

Never to stoop. Oh, sir, she smiled, no doubt,
Whene'er I passed her; but who passed without
Much the same smile? This grew; I gave commands;
Then all smiles stopped together. There she stands
As if alive. Will 't please you rise? We'll meet

What the duke wants from the envoy is presented as a question: 'Will't please you sit?' and 'Will't please you rise', but these are not questions at all. They are demands. The duke frames his demands as questions but, make no mistake, this is a social superior demanding something from an inferior. He is a **controlling** character.

The company below then. I repeat,
The Count your master's known munificence
Is ample warrant that no just pretence
Of mine for dowry will be disallowed;
Though his fair daughter's self, as I avowed
At starting, is my object. Nay, we'll go
Together down, sir. Notice Neptune, though,
Taming a sea-horse, thought a rarity,
Which Claus of Innsbruck cast in bronze for me!

As you can see, the language employed by Browning suggests that the duke is proud, possessive, controlling, vain, condescending, disingenuous, self-obsessed and irrational. Now let's move on to the form and structure of the poem.

It's interesting to note that the poem is free from almost any poetic imagery such as simile and metaphor. This matches Browning's form—a realistic conversation isn't filled with similes, metaphors, etc. However, there are some example of poetic devices in the poem.

The painting, hidden behind a curtain which only the duke pulls back, is a metaphor for the control the duke wishes to have. In life, the duchess smiling at everyone and everything caused the duke great distress. Now, with the smiling wife behind a curtain, the duke can keep the smiles just for himself. Again, this symbolises the control the duke wishes to have over his past (and future) wives.

The sculpture of Neptune taming a sea-horse is a metaphor for the domination the duke wishes to have over his wife. Neptune, the Roman god of the sea, was regularly portrayed as a strong, muscular man. In this sculpture, he is taming a wild creature, which reflects how the duke sees his role over his wives.

Form

'My Last Duchess' is an example of a dramatic monologue, which means the poem contains a single person who gives a speech to someone else. However, the speaker is not the poet, and the listener is silent throughout. Essentially, it means that we are listening to a one-way conversation. This is a form that allows us to identify the speaker's character from what they say. Usually, the reader works as a detective to analyse clues that reveal key details about the speaker, in this case the Duke of Ferrara. There is a gap between what the speaker wants us to know and what the reader can read between the lines.

The poem is written entirely in iambic pentameter, with ten syllables per line and every other syllable being stressed. The rhyme scheme is also tightly controlled, with the whole poem consisting of rhyming couplets. This tightly controlled form and structure reflects the tight control of the speaker.

Structure

As already explained, the poem is written in rhyming couplets. This tight control of structure reflects the tight control of the duke over his wife. However, the poem also contains enjambment where sentences don't finish at the end of each line but run over onto other lines. There are a number of reasons why the poet employs enjambment. Firstly, the poem is supposed to be real speech and, if the couplets stopped at the end of each line, this would sound mechanical and not at all like real dialogue. An alternative interpretation is that the enjambment reflects the duke's lack of self-control. Although he does everything he can to control others (reflected in the tightly controlled rhyming couplets and iambic pentameter), the enjambment shows the reader that he cannot control himself. The image created is one of a crazy man who cannot control his outbursts.

It is interesting to note that the poem contains one long, sprawling verse. Why is this? Firstly, the structure suggests that the duke does not stop to think about what he is saying—he simply gives his own explanation of events. He cares not for his listener, but spouts out his thoughts in a stream of consciousness. Secondly, we should consider the effect on the reader. When we read the whole poem aloud with no major breaks or pauses, we are overwhelmed by the immensity of the poem. This overwhelming aspect reflects how the duke himself is an overwhelming character.

Language Ambiguity

Some lines in the poem are ambiguous: the reader is unsure of the intended meaning. An example of this in the line 'I gave commands.' The reader infers that the duke commanded the death of his wife, but it is ambiguous, as we cannot be sure. However, Browning did give an interview in which he explained 'Yes, I meant that the commands were that she be put to death'.

More ambiguity is found in the speaker's description of the painting looking 'as if she were alive'. This could simply mean that the painting is life-like, or it could suggest that she is no longer alive.

When the duke explains that 'her looks went everywhere', the reader is left wondering if he is implying that his wife was promiscuous.

Alternative Interpretation

It is possible to read the poem as a portrayal of the duke's weakness, not power. His insecurity can be seen in his comment that 'her looks went everywhere'. Similarly, his sprawling monologue seems uncontrolled and careless. But even if we read the poem at face value, the duke still appears to be weak. Why is it so important to the duke that he has control over his wife?

Browning's poem can be read as a statement that Victorian men are weakened by their dependency on the power they have over women. It can be argued that Victorian men saw their wives as a reflection of themselves, but that this disempowered them.

Of course, we never hear the wife's side of the story. Her silenced voice again reflects the absolute control that the duke has. Furthermore, this reflects the Victorian society in which the poem was written, in that women were effectively silenced through their inability to vote, testify in court, etc. In this way, the duke's desire to control his wife's behaviour can be read as a metaphor for Victorian society's obsession with the behaviour and reputation of women. The fact that the Duchess did not reserve her 'smiles' for her husband alone is a huge problem for the Duke. In the same way, Victorian women were considered to be failures if they did not give up their will to their husbands.

PERCY BYSSHE SHELLEY'S 'OZYMANDIAS'
The Poet

Percy Shelley is one of the most interesting poets who ever lived! Although we should only study areas of a poet's life that are important to our understanding of their poetry, with Shelley, it's just too interesting not to look at everything:

1. He was born in 1792
2. Unlike Browning, Shelley is classified as a Romantic poet.
3. He came from a wealthy family.
4. He was set to inherit riches and become a politician.
5. He went to Eton and Oxford University.
6. He was expelled from university because he wrote in favour of atheism.
7. He eloped and married a 16-year-old.
8. He left his wife and ran off with Mary Wollstonecraft Godwin, author of 'Frankenstein' and daughter of Mary Wollstonecraft.
9. In 1816, his wife committed suicide; three weeks later, he married Mary, who took his surname and became Mary Shelley.
10. He drowned, aged 29, whilst sailing to Italy.

See? I told you he was a fascinating person! It's also interesting to note that Shelley was not very successful as a writer during his own lifetime. He was associated with the much more successful poets Byron and Keats, but was nowhere near as popular. While

Byron sold as many as 10,000 copies of his poetry in just one day, Shelley wrote almost for himself, with no major interest from the public. However, today he is regarded as one of the finest poets ever.

Shelley was a deeply political person. He was a pacifist who believed in nonviolent protest. He was also a vegetarian, writing widely on the subject.

Context

King George III

Shelley wrote 'Ozymandias' during the reign of King George III. A lot can be said about this king, who reigned for longer than any other before him. However, the key points for this poem are that King George III was involved in a great number of military conflicts around the globe. Shelley hated oppressive monarchical government and felt that a revolution was needed to overthrow it.

As we have seen, a writer will sometimes set their text in a different place to that in which they live. Shelley deliberately sets his poem in the 'distant land' of Egypt, supposedly criticising Pharaoh Ozymandias. Shelley begins 'Ozymandias' by detaching himself from the story being told. This creates a distancing effect, which makes his criticism subtler and less obvious: he immediately wants to make the point that he is not openly criticising British monarchy, yet the poem is clearly a thinly-veiled attack. While he appears to be criticising the pharaoh, Shelley is actually criticising King George III.

Ramesses

It is useful to know a little about Ramesses II (also known as Ozymandias).

Ozymandias was an Egyptian pharaoh who ruled from 1279 - 1213 BC. He is believed to be the Egyptian pharaoh who ruled during the Biblical exodus of Moses. Crucially, he led many battles to protect and extend the borders of Egypt. In this way, it is possible to compare him with King George III.

Shelley crafted this poem as part of a sonnet writing competition with his friend Horace Smith. Both wrote sonnets about Ozymandias, and both poems were eventually published. The real-life inspiration for the poem is believed to be a statue of Ramesses II that the British Museum had recently announced it would acquire. Weighing nearly eight tonnes, the fragment of Ramesses' head and torso dated back to the 13th century BC.

Romanticism

Shelley belonged to what is known as the second generation of Romantic poets. Romantic poetry can be defined as containing a number of conventions:

1. A dislike of urban life, embracing instead the natural world
2. A love of the supernatural
3. Use of ordinary, everyday language

The most famous early Romantics are Wordsworth and Coleridge. However, by the time Shelley was writing, it was felt that the early Romantics had sold out—Wordsworth, for example, was now working as a taxman! So, the second generation of Romantics had to set themselves apart from the old guard. Byron, Shelley and Keats therefore looked to antiquity and foreign lands as the settings of their poetry to distinguish themselves from what had gone before. Of course, we see this in 'Ozymandias', which is set in a foreign land and refers to an ancient historical period. These second-generation Romantic poets often wrote against religion and political control. They used rich language that was full of metaphor and classical allusion.

The Literal Meaning

Now we know about the poet and the context, let's look at a simple translation of the poem itself.

Original	Translation
I met a traveller from an antique land *Who said: `Two vast and trunkless legs of stone* *Stand in the desert.* *Near them, on the sand,* *Half sunk, a shattered visage lies, whose frown,* *And wrinkled lip, and sneer of cold command,* *Tell that its sculptor well those passions read* *Which yet survive, stamped on these lifeless things,* *The hand that mocked them and the heart that fed.* *And on the pedestal these words appear—* *"My name is Ozymandias, king of kings:* *Look on my works, ye Mighty, and despair!"* *Nothing beside remains. Round the decay* *Of that colossal wreck, boundless and bare* *The lone and level sands stretch far away.'*	I met a traveller from an historic land Who told me there were two huge stone legs Standing in the desert. Near the legs, on the sand, Sunk into the ground a bit, there lay the head of the statue, Its face shattered and cracked. It has a nasty look on its face, looking powerful. The artist made it very life-like. And at the foot of the statue is an engraving reading "My name is Ozymandias, king above all kings: Look at all I have achieved, you great ones, and feel hopeless!" Nothing else remains, around the broken Statue, isolated in The middle of the lonely desert.

Themes

The major theme of 'Ozymandias' is that those with power are deluded in their belief that their power is supreme and invincible. The might and power of leaders does not last, but art (as represented by the statue) does. Even then, nature conquers it. It is also possible to read the poem as a criticism of Christianity and religious belief in general.

Now that we understand the themes of the poem, it's time to analyse the language, structure and form to detect where those themes are present and how they are explored by the poet.

The Form: Sonnet

'Ozymandias' is a sonnet. The sonnet is a genre of love poetry which originated in Italy in the 13th century. The 14th-century poet Petrarch is the most recognised Italian sonneteer. Falling in love with a woman known only as 'Laura', he wrote 366 sonnets to her. Despite his literary outpourings, she rejected his proposals.

Like the Shakespearean (or Elizabethan) sonnet, a Petrarchan (or Italian) sonnet has 14 lines. Both sonnet forms are written in iambic pentameter (lines of 10 syllables, with alternating stressed and unstressed syllables).

The structure of a Petrarchan sonnet is different, however:

- The first 8 lines (known as the octave) present a problem
- The last 6 lines (known as the sestet) present a solution to the problem
- Line 9 (known as the volta) introduces a sharp twist or turn, which brings about the move to the resolution
- The octave has an ABBAABBA rhyme scheme.
- The rhyme scheme of the sestet will vary

The Shakespearean Sonnet

In the 16th century, the sonnet made its way into English poetry. Sir Philip Sidney developed it, but it came to be known as the Shakespearean sonnet after Shakespeare made it truly famous. This form is quite different to the Petrarchan sonnet:

- It is divided into 3 verses of four lines each, known as quatrains, and finished with a rhyming couplet which also serves as the volta.
- Its rhyme scheme is also different: ABAB CDCD EFEF GG.

However, the topic of Shakespearean sonnets (also called Elizabethan sonnets) remains the same: they are all about love.

Which type of Sonnet is 'Ozymandias'?

Interestingly, 'Ozymandias' is a mixture of the Petrarchan and Shakespearean sonnet forms. As a Petrarchan sonnet, it follows the format of having an octave that presents details about the powerful Ozymandias as represented through his broken statue. The sestet then focuses on how the power of Ozymandias has disappeared—nature outliving the powerful ruler.

Secondly, there are elements of the Shakespearean sonnet in the poem's form. Consider the rhyme scheme of these first four lines:

> I met a traveller from an antique land
> Who said: `Two vast and trunkless legs of stone
> Stand in the desert. Near them, on the sand,
> Half sunk, a shattered visage lies, whose frown,

Here we see the rhyme scheme ABAB (*land, stone, sand, frown*). This, then, is evidence of the Shakespearean sonnet. But it doesn't stop there! The rhyme scheme then changes:

> And wrinkled lip, and sneer of cold command,
> Tell that its sculptor well those passions read
> Which yet survive, stamped on these lifeless things,
> The hand that mocked them and the heart that fed.
> And on the pedestal these words appear --
> "My name is Ozymandias, king of kings:
> Look on my works, ye Mighty, and despair!"
> Nothing beside remains. Round the decay
> Of that colossal wreck, boundless and bare
> The lone and level sands stretch far away.'

Now the rhyme scheme becomes ABABACDCEDEFEF. This, then, is a 'new' structure for the sonnet. It is key to our understanding of the poem.

As we have established, the major theme of the poem is how those with power are deluded in their belief that their power is supreme and invincible. Shelley's clever use of form here suggests the same thing—just as Petrarch's sonnet form gave way to Shakespeare's, then (in this poem) Shakespeare's form gives way to the 'new' form. This symbolises that all power ultimately gives way to new power. Nothing remains forever: not even the form of the sonnet.

It is also worth considering why the sonnet form is employed in the first place. Remember, sonnets are exclusively poems about love. Perhaps Shelley uses this form to point out that Ozymandias (and the arrogant rulers he represents) are in love with themselves.

Language

Now let's analyse the language used by Shelley. When analysing language, we are looking for any occasion where words seem to have been deliberately chosen by the poet for effect.

Ozymandias

'Ozy' comes from the Greek 'Ozium', meaning 'to breathe'. 'Mandias' comes from the Greek 'mandate', meaning 'to rule'. Even the title suggests power and control.

> *I met a traveller from an antique land*
> *Who said: `Two vast and trunkless legs of stone*
> *Stand in the desert. Near them, on the sand,*

Shelley begins 'Ozymandias' by detaching himself from the story being told. He wants to immediately make the point this is not an open criticism of the British monarchy. However, the poem is clearly a thinly-veiled attack.

> *Half sunk, a shattered visage lies, whose frown,*

This deeply negative language is used to make it very clear that the poem is an attack on the powerful. Its intention is not to praise.

> *And wrinkled lip, and sneer of cold command,*

The alliterative repetition of the hard 'c' sounds reflects the harsh nature of Ozymandias.

> *Tell that its sculptor well those passions read*
> *Which yet survive, stamped on these lifeless things,*
> *The hand that mocked them and the heart that fed.*
> *And on the pedestal these words appear --*
> *"My name is Ozymandias, king of kings:*

Here's one of the religious references I will explore a little later.

> *Look on my works, ye Mighty, and despair!"*
> *Nothing beside remains. Round the decay*
> *Of that colossal wreck, boundless and bare*

Alliteration is used to emphasise the emptiness.

> *The lone and level sands stretch far away.'*

The desert outlives the statue.

One of the key skills to demonstrate in your English literature exam is the ability to offer perceptive and original analysis. Put simply, this means that you need to stand out from the other students. Your examiner will be marking hundreds of papers, and your job is to be a rare gem in the pile. One of the simple ways to achieve this is to analyse form and structure rather than language. Most students analyse language in their answers, as this is the easiest approach to poetry. However, as the following sample answer demonstrates, it is possible to analyse form and structure.

EXAMPLE POWER AND CONFLICT QUESTION

Compare how poets present ideas about power in Shelley's 'Ozymandias' and one other poem.

[30 marks]

EXAMPLE ANSWER

In both Shelley's 'Ozymandias' and Browning's 'My Last Duchess', the poets use form to present power as being eternal and domineering. However, both poets then use structure to undermine these assertions.

In 'Ozymandias', the statue itself asserts that the 'king of kings' will have eternal power. Shelley employs the sonnet form of classic love poetry to reflect the self-obsessed nature of the powerful. Just as the poetic form is all about love, Ozymandias is full of love for himself. However, Shelley uses structure to undermine this notion of the eternal nature of power.

Interestingly, 'Ozymandias' is a mixture of the classic Petrarchan and more modern Shakespearean sonnet forms. As a Petrarchan sonnet, it follows the form of having an octave that presents details about the powerful Ozymandias as represented through his 'shattered visage'. The sestet then focuses on how the power of Ozymandias has disappeared into the 'lone and level sands', as nature outlives the powerful ruler.

However, there are also elements of the much later Shakespearean sonnet in the poem's form. Consider the rhyme scheme of these first four lines. Here we see the rhyme scheme ABAB ('land', 'stone', 'sand', 'frown'). This, then, is evidence of the Shakespearean sonnet. At this point, Shelley has moved from the classic 13th-century model to the popular 16th-century form. But it doesn't end there. In the rest of the poem, the rhyme scheme changes again, to ABABACDCEDEFEF. This, then, is a 'new' structure for the sonnet. Shelley has used three different sonnet forms in this one poem: the classic Petrarchan form, the famous Shakespearean form and a third, new, inventive form. The major theme of the poem is how those with power are deluded in their belief that their power is supreme and invincible. Shelley's clever use of form here suggests the same thing: just as Petrarch's sonnet form gave way to Shakespeare's, and Shakespeare's form gives way to the 'new' form, all power ultimately gives way to new power. Nothing remains forever—power is not invincible.

Similarly, Browning employs form to convey his message about power being dominant. In 'My Last Duchess', the power in question is male power over women. 'My Last Duchess' is an example of a dramatic monologue where the poem contains a single person, the duke, who gives a speech to someone else. However, the speaker is not the poet, and the listener is silent throughout. Thus, we never actually hear from the envoy, who is asked to 'sit and look'. Of course, we also never hear the wife's side of the story—this silenced voice again reflects the duke's absolute control. This use of form reflects Browning's message about the power men had over women, so much so that their voices were silenced. The lack of voice from the duchess presents the duke's power as complete and domineering.

To further enforce this presentation of power, the poem is written entirely in iambic pentameter with ten syllables per line and every other syllable being stressed. The rhyme scheme is also tightly controlled, with the whole poem consisting of rhyming couplets such as 'wall' and 'call'. This tightly controlled form and structure reflects the tight control of the speaker: it reflects the notion that power is exhibited through complete control and dominance.

However, just as Ozymandias clearly wanted eternal power but failed to get it, there is a sense that the narrator of 'My Last Duchess' fails to achieve the power and control he also wishes to have. As already explained, the poem is written in rhyming couplets and this tight control of structure reflects the tight control of the duke over his wife. However, the poem also contains enjambment, where sentences do not finish at the end of each line but run over onto other lines. We see this throughout the poem:

> Looking as if she were alive. I call
> That piece a wonder, now;

This use of enjambment reflects the nature of the duke. Although he does everything he can to control others (reflected in the tightly controlled rhyming couplets and iambic pentameter), the fact is that he cannot control himself is seen through the enjambment. The image created is one of a crazy man who cannot control his outbursts. So, in both poems, structural devices are used to undermine the idea that power is eternal and domineering.

Also, both poems contain one long verse. In 'Ozymandias', this is because it is following the conventions of a sonnet and therefore must contain one verse. However, this is not the case in 'My Last Duchess'. Firstly, Browning's use of structure suggests that the duke does not stop to think about what is saying—he simply gives his own explanation of events. He cares not for his listener, but spouts out his thoughts in a stream of consciousness style. Alternatively, when we read the whole poem aloud with no major breaks or pauses, we are overwhelmed by the immensity of the poem. This overwhelming aspect reflects how the duke himself is an overwhelming character.

To conclude, both poets employ structure and form to present their ideas about power. In 'Ozymandias', the proud assertion that power remains forever is disproven. In 'My Last Duchess', the notion of male power over women is presented and subtly undermined.

How to Analyse Poetry: Love and Relationships

Let's look at a typical question based on the Love and Relationships cluster:

> Compare how poets present attitudes towards a loved one in Elizabeth Barrett Browning's 'Sonnet XXIX' and one other poem.
>
> **[30 marks]**

The way to approach this question is to begin by looking at the named poem–in this case, 'Sonnet XXIX':

Sonnet XXIX

I think of thee !—my thoughts do twine and bud
About thee, as wild vines, about a tree,
Put out broad leaves, and soon there 's nought to see
Except the straggling green which hides the wood.
Yet, O my palm-tree, be it understood
I will not have my thoughts instead of thee
Who art dearer, better ! Rather, instantly
Renew thy presence; as a strong tree should,
Rustle thy boughs and set thy trunk all bare,
And let these bands of greenery which insphere thee
Drop heavily down,—burst, shattered, everywhere !
Because, in this deep joy to see and hear thee
And breathe within thy shadow a new air,
I do not think of thee—I am too near thee.

Before choosing the second poem, it's important to pick out a few key points you might make about the named poem. 'Sonnet XXIX' was written by the poet to the man she was engaged to marry. In it, she expresses the idea that thinking of her future husband is such an intense feeling that it ultimately overpowers her.

It is useful to take the wording of the question and put it into a phrase:

> *The attitude towards love that we find in 'Sonnet XXIX' is one of the overwhelming feelings felt when the speaker is apart from her loved one.*

With this in mind, we can now consider which one seems to compare well. Because we are comparing, we are ideally looking for a poem that has some similarities but also some notable differences. A good choice seems to be 'When We Two Parted' by Byron:

When We Two Parted

When we two parted
In silence and tears,
Half broken-hearted
To sever for years,
Pale grew thy cheek and cold,

Colder thy kiss;
Truly that hour foretold
Sorrow to this.

The dew of the morning
Sank chill on my brow—
It felt like the warning
Of what I feel now.
Thy vows are all broken,
And light is thy fame;
I hear thy name spoken,
And share in its shame.

They name thee before me,
A knell in mine ear;
A shudder come o'er me—
Why wert thou so dear?
They know not I knew thee,
Who knew thee too well—
Long, long shall I rue thee,
Too deeply to tell.

In secret we met—
In silence I grieve,
That thy heart could forget,
Thy spirit deceive.
If I should meet thee
After long years,
How should I greet thee?—
With silence and tears.

'When We Two Parted' is a poem focusing on Byron's love for a married woman by the name of Lady Frances Wedderburn Webster. Apparently, he found out that she was having an affair with the Duke of Wellington. In this poem, he remembers his pain at losing the woman he loved.

So, there is definitely a line of comparison in the fact that both poems focus on the pain endured when apart from the one you love. However, 'Sonnet XXIX' focuses on feelings for a future husband whereas 'When We Two Parted' looks at a love affair. This therefore seems a good choice of comparison, as there are similarities and differences in the poems.

Let's take a closer look at 'Sonnet XXIX'.

SONNET XXIX
The Poet

When it comes to biographical detail, it is important that we only look at the details of a poet's life that are relevant to the poem itself. Therefore, the following details should be considered:

- Elizabeth Barrett was born in 1806 and died in 1861.
- She was a very successful poet, who was published from the age of 15.
- She suffered great sickness and invalidity for her entire adult life.
- She was famous in both the UK and USA during her lifetime.
- The poet Robert Browning wrote to her as a fan and ended up becoming her husband.
- Elizabeth Barrett Browning was a deeply Christian woman.

The Form: Sonnet

The sonnet is a genre of love poetry which originated in Italy in the 13th century. The 14th-century poet Petrarch is the most recognised Italian sonneteer. Falling in love with a woman known only as 'Laura', he wrote 366 sonnets to her. Despite his literary outpourings, she rejected his proposals.

All sonnets have 14 lines. They are also both written in iambic pentameter (lines of 10 syllables, with alternating stressed and unstressed syllables).

Structure of a Petrarchan (or Italian) Sonnet

The structure of a Petrarchan sonnet, named after Petrarch, is as follows:

- The first 8 lines (known as the octave) present a problem
- The last 6 lines (known as the sestet) present a solution to the problem
- Line 9 (known as the volta) introduces a sharp twist, or turn, which brings about the move to the resolution
- The octave has an ABBAABBA rhyme scheme.
- The rhyme scheme of the sestet will vary.

Structure of a Shakespearean (or Elizabethan) Sonnet

In the 16th Century, the sonnet made its way into English poetry. Sir Philip Sidney developed it, but it came to be known as the **Shakespearean sonnet** after Shakespeare made it truly famous. This form is quite different to the Petrarchan sonnet:

- It is divided into 3 verses of four lines each, known as quatrains, and finished with a rhyming couplet which also serves as the volta.
- Its rhyme scheme is also different: ABAB CDCD EFEF GG.

However, the topic of Shakespearean sonnets remains the same: they are all about love.

Browning's 'Sonnet XXIX' follows the conventions of the Petrarchan sonnet; perhaps Browning related to Petrarch's intense spiritual feelings of pre-marital love and shied away from Shakespeare's poetry that was more experienced in love and sometimes overtly sexual.

The Context: 'Sonnets from the Portuguese'

During their engagement, Elizabeth wrote 44 sonnets to Robert Browning, her husband-to-be. Robert was so impressed with the sonnets that he encouraged Elizabeth to publish them. However, the sonnets were deeply personal, and Elizabeth would only agree to publish them anonymously. She didn't want anyone to know that they were written by her.

'Sonnets from the Portuguese' was published in 1850, promoted as an English translation of a collection of Portuguese poems. The 'Portuguese' part is a nod to Luis De Camoes, a Portuguese sonneteer, whom Elizabeth admired greatly. 'My little Portuguese' was also Robert's nickname for Elizabeth.

Analysing Form

'Sonnet XXIX' follows the Petrarchan sonnet form, but there are some notable differences. To begin with, the poem employs iambic pentameter, but it occasionally breaks this convention. Consider line three:

> *Put out broad leaves, and soon there's nought to see*

In this line, we have three stressed syllables in a row with the words 'out broad leaves'. Why is this? Perhaps Barrett Browning is suggesting how powerful and intense her thoughts are at this moment. Here we can see that the poet is deliberately playing with the form to express her feelings about the intensity of love. Linking back to the question, we might write it into an exam answer like this:

SAMPLE ANALYSIS OF FORM AND STRUCTURE

Barrett Browning presents love as intense and overwhelming in the poem 'Sonnet XXIX'. The poem is a sonnet, following the conventions of the Petrarchan sonnet. However, there are occasions when the poet deliberately subverts the form. In line three, there are three stressed syllables in a row, where the poet describes how she will put 'out broad leaves'. This line is used to describe the all-encompassing and all-consuming intensity of the poet's thoughts. By breaking the sonnet conventions, we are given a sense of how overwhelming these feelings are. Just as the thoughts can overpower the poet, they can also overpower the form of the poem itself, forcing it beyond its limits.

Analysing Structure

Now let's consider the structure of the poem. A sonnet should have its volta (a change between the octave and sestet) in line eight. However, in 'Sonnet XXIX' we find the volta straddled between lines 7 and 8:

> *Rather, instantly*
> *Renew thy presence;*

So why does Barrett Browning deliberately break some of the rules? Well, if the sonnet is a poem about perfect love, perhaps Barrett Browning refuses to follow the form perfectly to reflect how the love she has for Browning is not perfect and will not be so until the two are together. In other words, *I can't write the perfect love poem because my love is not perfect: he is not here, with me.*

These types of points are complex and difficult, but a close study of each poem will reveal something in this area.

'WHEN WE TWO PARTED'
Form and Structure

'When We Two Parted' is an example of accentual verse. This means that each line must contain the same number of stressed syllables, no matter how many syllables there are in each line. Sound confusing? Let's look at an example:

When we two parted
In silence and tears,
Half broken-hearted
To sever for years,
Pale grew thy cheek and cold,
Colder thy kiss;
Truly that hour foretold
Sorrow to this.

Here we see that there are two stressed syllables per line, even though the lines themselves have anywhere between 4 and 6 syllables, but the stressed syllable count remains at 2. However, look at lines 5 - 8:

Lines	Underlined stressed Syllables	Syllables
5	<u>Pale</u> grew thy <u>cheek</u> and <u>cold</u>,	3
6	<u>Colder</u> thy <u>kiss</u>;	2
7	<u>Truly</u> that <u>hour</u> fore<u>told</u>	3
8	<u>Sorrow</u> to <u>this</u>	2

Lines 5 and 7 break the rules of accentuated verse, containing 3 stressed syllables. Like Barrett Browning, Byron is breaking the rules of form and structure, and he is doing so to make an important point.

The line 'Pale grew thy cheek and cold' describes the moment when the poet was rejected by his lover. This woman, whom he had loved, was turning 'cold' on him. This action made the poet feel broken and rejected, thus the poem structure is 'broken' too.

So how would we add this to our exam style answer? How about this:

EXAMPLE QUESTION

Compare how poets present attitudes towards a loved one in Elizabeth Barrett Browning's 'Sonnet XXIX' and one other poem.

SAMPLE COMPARATIVE ANALYSIS OF FORM AND STRUCTURE

In 'Sonnet XXIX', Elizabeth Barrett Browning presents love as intense and overwhelming. The poem is a sonnet, following the conventions of the Petrarchan sonnet form. However, there are occasions when the poet deliberately subverts the form. The poem mostly follows the sonnet convention of iambic pentameter, but on occasion it does not. In line three, there are three stressed syllables in a row, where the poet describes how she will put 'out broad leaves'. This line specifically describes the all-consuming intensity of the poet's thoughts. By breaking the sonnet convention, we are given a sense of how overwhelming these feelings of love are. Just as the thoughts overpower the poet, they also overpower the form of the poem itself, forcing it to breaking point.

Similarly, Byron breaks the conventions of his chosen poetic form in the poem 'When We Two Parted'. This poem is an example of accentuated verse, with each line containing two stressed syllables and any number of unstressed syllables. However, this is not the case in line 5 in which the poet is shocked with 'pale grew thy cheek and cold'. In this line, the words 'pale', 'cheek' and 'cold' are stressed, and the poet is describing the moment that he was rejected by his lover. This woman, whom he had loved, was turning 'cold' on him. This action made the poet feel broken and rejected, thus the poem structure is 'broken' too. Both Barrett Browning and Byron deliberately break the form of their poems to show the intensity that can be caused by love.

Analysing Language

Of course, the mark scheme requires language **and** structure **and** form, so it's important to look at the language too. To me, there are some interesting points to be made about the religious language in 'Sonnet XXIX':

> *I think of thee !--my thoughts do twine and bud*
> *About thee, as wild vines, about a tree,*

Here, the poet describes her future husband as a tree, and herself as a vine. This is reminiscent of the words of Jesus in John 15:5:

> *I am the vine, ye are the branches: He that abideth in me, and I in him, the same bringeth forth much fruit: for without me ye can do nothing.*

Jesus is here saying that he is the tree; his followers are its branches. The image of the tree symbolises the notion that Christians can do nothing if not connected to God. In 'Sonnet XXIX', the poet describes Browning, her future husband, as 'a tree'. In fact, there is a plethora of religious imagery in the poem. When the poet calls Browning 'my palm-tree', she is referencing the Song of Solomon in the Bible. The Song of Solomon is a poem about the sexual love between a man and his bride. Consider the striking similarities here:

> *I said, I will go up to the palm tree, I will take hold of the boughs thereof: now also thy breasts shall be as clusters of the vine, and the smell of thy nose like apples (Song of Solomon, 7:8).*

The use of 'palm tree' and 'bough' is certainly taken from Song of Solomon, but why? As a deeply religious woman, Barrett Browning is here pointing out that she is looking forward to sex in the context of marriage. The references to Song of Solomon are a reminder that God created sex to be enjoyed between husband and wife. There is a sense that sexual attraction between husband and wife is right, honourable and pure. This is not something we see in the Byron poem. In fact, Byron is bereft of religious imagery because the relationship he is writing of—an affair with a married woman—is not right, honourable or pure. So, if there is no religious imagery, what is there?

'When We Two Parted' is filled with sensory description. From the sound imagery of 'hear' and 'knell' to the touch imagery of 'colder' and 'shudder', the poem focuses on the language of sensory description. Could this be Byron's way of pointing out that the relationship was about sensory pleasure? There was no sacred or religious element to it. It was all about physical intimacy. If so, how could we write these two conflicting ideas about the nature of love into our exam answer?

SAMPLE COMPARATIVE ANALYSIS OF LANGUAGE

Barrett Browning uses language to suggest that love is a pure and religious experience. Many of the images are intertextual references from the Song of Solomon in the Bible. When the poet explains that her 'thoughts do twine and bud about thee, as wild vines, about a tree', there are two obvious Biblical allusions being made. Barrett Browning describes her future husband as a tree and herself as a vine. This is reminiscent of the words of Jesus in John 15:5:

I am the vine, ye are the branches: He that abideth in me, and I in him, the same bringeth forth much fruit: for without me ye can do nothing.

Jesus is here saying that he is the tree; his followers are its branches. The image of the tree symbolises the notion that Christians can do nothing if not connected to God. In 'Sonnet XXIX', the poet describes Browning, her future lover, as 'a tree'. What this tells us about the nature of love is that a loved one is so important that they can become godlike in the eyes of their lover.

In fact, there is a plethora of religious imagery in the poem. When the poet calls Browning 'my palm-tree', she is referencing the Song of Solomon in the Bible. The Song of Solomon is a poem about the sexual love between a man and his bride. As a deeply religious woman, Barrett Browning is here pointing out that she is looking forward to sex in the context of marriage. The references to Song of Solomon are a reminder that God created sex to be enjoyed between husband and wife. There is a sense that sexual attraction between husband and wife is right, honourable and pure. The use of religious language symbolises that love is sexual and passionate, and that there is nothing wrong with that in the context of marriage.

This is not something we see in the Byron poem. In fact, Byron is bereft of religious imagery because the relationship he is writing of—an affair with a married woman—is not right, honourable or pure in the eyes of religion. Byron uses language to show us that love is a physical feeling and desire, not a religious one. 'When We Two Parted' is filled with sensory description. From the sound imagery of 'hear' and 'knell' to the touch imagery of 'colder' and 'shudder', the poem focuses on the language of sensory description. This is Byron's way of pointing out that the relationship was about sensory pleasure, not religious connection. There was no sacred or religious element to it: it was all about physical intimacy.

OK, let's put all that together and see what our final exam answer looks like:

FINAL EXAM ANSWER:

In 'Sonnet XXIX', Elizabeth Barrett Browning presents love as intense and overwhelming. The poem is a sonnet, following the conventions of the Petrarchan sonnet form. However, there are occasions when the poet deliberately subverts the form. The poem mostly follows the sonnet convention of iambic pentameter, but on occasion it does not. In line three, there are three stressed syllables in a row, where the poet describes how she will put 'out broad leaves'. This line specifically describes the all-consuming intensity of the poet's thoughts. By breaking the sonnet convention, we are given a sense of how overwhelming these feelings of love are. Just as the thoughts overpower the poet, they also overpower the form of the poem itself, forcing it to breaking point.

Similarly, Byron breaks the conventions of his chosen poetic form in the poem 'When We Two Parted'. This poem is an example of accentuated verse, with each line containing two stressed syllables and any number of unstressed syllables. However, this is not the case in line 5 in which the poet is shocked with 'pale grew thy cheek and cold'. In this line, the words 'pale', 'cheek' and 'cold' are stressed, and the poet is describing the moment that he was rejected by his lover. This woman, whom he had loved, was turning 'cold' on him. This action made the poet feel broken and rejected, thus the poem structure is 'broken' too. Both Barrett Browning and Byron deliberately break the form of their poems to show the intensity that can be caused by love.

Barrett Browning uses language to suggest that love is a pure and religious experience. Many of the images are intertextual references from the Song of Solomon in the Bible. When the poet explains that her 'thoughts do twine and bud about thee, as wild vines, about a tree', there are two obvious Biblical allusions being made. Barrett Browning describes her future husband as a tree and herself as a vine. This is reminiscent of the words of Jesus in John 15:5:

I am the vine, ye are the branches: He that abideth in me, and I in him, the same bringeth forth much fruit: for without me ye can do nothing.

Jesus is here saying that he is the tree; his followers are its branches. The image of the tree symbolises the notion that Christians can do nothing if not connected to God. In 'Sonnet XXIX', the poet describes Browning, her future lover, as 'a tree'. What this tells us about the nature of love is that a loved one is so important that they can become godlike in the eyes of their lover.

In fact, there is a plethora of religious imagery in the poem. When the poet calls Browning 'my palm-tree', she is referencing the Song of Solomon in the Bible. The Song of Solomon is a poem about the sexual love between a man and his bride. As a deeply religious woman, Barrett Browning is here pointing out that she is looking forward to sex in the context of marriage. The references to Song of Solomon are a reminder that God created sex to be enjoyed between husband and wife. There is a sense that sexual attraction between husband and wife is right, honourable and pure. The use of religious language symbolises that love is sexual and passionate, and that there is nothing wrong with that in the context of marriage.

This is not something we see in the Byron poem. In fact, Byron is bereft of religious imagery because the relationship he is writing of—an affair with a married woman—is not right, honourable or pure in the eyes of religion. Byron uses language to show us that love is a physical feeling and desire, not a religious one. 'When We Two Parted' is filled with sensory description. From the sound imagery of 'hear' and 'knell' to the touch imagery of 'colder' and 'shudder', the poem focuses on the language of sensory description. This is Byron's way of pointing out that the relationship was about sensory pleasure, not religious connection. There was no sacred or religious element to it: it was all about physical intimacy.

Although these poems are complex, the exam answers do what we've been doing all along: they analyse language, structure and form, weaving in our knowledge of context as and when appropriate.

Language Paper 2, Section C: Unseen Poetry

In Section C, you will be asked to:

1. Analyse an unseen poem (24 marks available).
2. Compare a second unseen poem to the first unseen poem (8 marks available).

You will have just 45 minutes to plan and write your answers to both questions.

In terms of timing, I would recommend one-minute writing time per mark. Divide the remaining time for reading and planning. This would give you:

Task	Timing
Reading and planning response to unseen poem	8
Writing answer	24
Reading second unseen poem and planning comparative task	5
Writing answer	8
Total minutes:	45

First Unseen Poem (Section C, Question 1)

Let's take a look at an unseen poem and the question that follows:

BULLY
Your words cut into me, sharp as a knife
The pain that you cause always goes unseen
I curl up defenceless, scared for my life
Why do you always have to be so mean?

We met in our tutor group, class 8E
At first you barely saw that I was there
But soon your attention fell upon me
Your words were flying and always unfair

After a few years we became good friends
Most of the time, you were actually kind
But then those moments of friendship would end
The good times were gone – all kindness behind

But those very good times enriched my life
That's why in the end I took you as my wife

Andrew Smith
1981-

78

OK, here are five steps to follow with any unseen poem.

Step 1: Read for literal meaning

The exam board will choose a poem that has both a simple meaning and a complex meaning. To begin with, read through the poem and look for the simple meaning: what does this poem literally mean?

Using 'Bully' as an example, we can say that the poem is about two school enemies who later become friends and get married—that is the simple, literal meaning.

Step 2: Look for the poetic devices

You should really do this at the same time as step 3, but look for the poetic devices used in the poem. For example: similes, metaphors, alliteration, onomatopoeia, etc.

Step 3: Look at the structure and form

How is the poem organised? When do the verses change and why? Does it follow the pattern of a type of poetry? The poem 'Bully' follows the form of Shakespearean Sonnet. It is clear that Smith uses the sonnet form to back up the message that this poem is about falling in love (albeit with a childhood enemy).

Step 4: Second reading: look for the inconsistencies/deeper meanings

The next step is to look for the deeper meaning of the poem. This is often found by looking for words or phrases that don't seem to fit in with the literal interpretation. In the poem above, you might consider the use of the present tense use of the verb 'cause' which suggests that this bullying is still taking place to this day. Perhaps this poem is more than *we used to hate each-other and now we love each-other* and is actually about domestic abuse.

Similarly, the form of the poem suggests a deeper meaning. Although it follows the sonnet form religiously, the last line contains 11 syllables not 10. On first reading, this is a very happy line, which seems to laugh at the way the married couple used to be friends. However, why did Smith choose to break the sonnet form? Does it, perhaps, suggest that the couple's love is not real?

Step 5: Answer the question

In terms of timing, steps 1-4 should really only take 4 or 5 minutes to complete.

TOP TIPS FOR THE UNSEEN POETRY QUESTION
- Analyse language, structure and form
- Write in PEE paragraphs
- Write about the poet's themes and the effect on the reader

With all that in mind, let's look at some sample answers.

A 'GOOD' SAMPLE ANSWER:

The poet's attitude to relationships is that they are complex and multi-faceted. On the one hand, relationships are loving and romantic. This is seen through the use of the sonnet form. The poem follows the form of a Shakespearean sonnet: 14 lines of iambic pentameter with an ABAB CDCD EFEF GG rhyme scheme. By using the form of a famous type of love poetry, Smith is showing that the relationship is loving. However, the title of the poem tells another story. By calling the poem 'bully', it is clear that this relationship contains pain and suffering as well. This pain and suffering is also seen throughout the poem. The effect on the reader is that they may feel confused about these conflicting emotions, which is probably how Smith himself feels.

OK, so the above is good because it is structured into a PEE paragraph and comments on the effect on the reader. It analyses language and form, and shows a clear knowledge and understanding of sonnets. However, it only focuses on a surface analysis—there is much more that could be said. So, how do you develop that answer to gain more marks? Using the above answer as a starting point, let's see if we can develop it into something more sophisticated that addresses the deeper meanings and possible alternative interpretations.

A 'BETTER' SAMPLE ANSWER

The poet's attitude to relationships is that they are complex and multi-faceted. On the one hand, relationships are loving and romantic. This is seen through the use of the sonnet form. The poem follows the form of a Shakespearean sonnet: 14 lines of iambic pentameter with an ABAB CDCD EFEF GG rhyme scheme. By using the form of a famous type of love poetry, Smith is showing that the relationship is loving. However, the use of the sonnet form is more subversive in this poem—it isn't until the volta at the end when we actually realise this poem is about a marriage. The effect of this sharp twist on the reader is that they are surprised to see these seemingly combatant people are married. Perhaps Smith himself is surprised at how he has fallen into this marriage. Furthermore, it is very important to note that the poem is not a perfect sonnet—the last line 'That's why in the end I took you as my wife' contains 11 syllables when it should only contain 10. This suggests that there is more lurking under the surface of this seemingly happy marriage—perhaps it is not quite so happy at all, but is a façade, just like the forced and ultimately inaccurate use of the sonnet form.

The language of the poem certainly does little to suggest the relationship is a happy one. By calling the poem 'bully', it is clear that this relationship contains pain and suffering, which are clearly seen throughout the poem. In fact, in verse one there is a suggestion that the relationship is still not happy, seen in the present tense use of the verb 'cause'. This is perhaps a subtle hint that the 'bullying' of their childhood is still taking place in their modern marriage. In this interpretation, it could even be suggested that childhood bullying is a metaphor for domestic abuse. Smith might be covering the issue through childish imagery to reflect how he feels immature and childish to be the victim of domestic abuse and yet also be a man.

You can see that this answer is much more sophisticated than the first. It picks out subtleties and inconsistencies, analysing these persuasively. As with all poetry, you don't have to have the right answer: any answer is valid if it can be explained.

But don't rest just yet. You'll remember that the exam requires you to compare **two** unseen poems. Another 8-mark question will assess your understanding of a second poem and your ability to compare it with the one you have just analysed.

Second Unseen Poem (Section C, Question 1)
We're now going to pick apart a second unseen poem using the five-step process. Then I'll use it to provide another example response for the first 24-mark question.

MY LOVE FOR YOU

My love for you is strong and true,
I could not survive without you,
My love for you is real and strong,
I'll love you with laughter and with song,
My love for you will last forever,
It will not change is sun or bad weather,
My love for you is flying high,
It will last forever - my love will never die

> *Walt Chapman*
> *1942-1999*

Now let's apply the five-step process to this poem.

Step 1: Read for literal meaning

The poem is very simple, with one person telling another how much they love them.

Step 2: Look for the poetic devices

The whole poem is made up of rhyming couplets, but there is nothing in the way of similes, metaphors, etc. Again, the poem seems to be deliberately simple, perhaps to suggest a childlike and innocent love on the part of the speaker.

Step 3: Look at the structure and form

No sonnets here, but rhyming couplets all the way through. These could symbolise the two lovers.

The poem is a dramatic monologue: one person seems to be speaking to another, but we never hear from the person being addressed.

Step 4: Second reading: look for the inconsistencies/deeper meanings

Each couplet starts with 'my love for you', giving a sense of one-sidedness to the relationship

The couplets begin by containing the same number of syllables but, with each couplet, the second line gets longer and longer whereas the first line stays the same. This could suggest a growing apart in the relationship despite the passionate and heart-felt words of the speaker.

Step 5: Answer the question

ANSWERING THE QUESTION

EXAMPLE QUESTION 1:

In 'My Love for You', how does the poet present the lovers' relationship?

[24 marks]

The example below uses the five-step process. Once again, I should begin by writing about structure and form if possible—these are the most impressive points to make. I should structure my answer in PEE paragraphs, and make sure I am focusing on the key words in the question, not just writing everything I think about the poem.

SAMPLE ANSWER:

In 'My Love for You', Chapman uses structure and form to present the relationship as one-sided. The poet uses the form of a monologue, with the speaker continually telling the listener how much he loves her. The repetition of 'my love for you' suggests a sense of desperation and negativity, and it seems that the speaker's love is not matched by that of the listener. In this way, the use of a monologue form is perfect, as we never hear from the listener, and this leads us to question the equality of emotion in the poem. This notion is further enforced by the use of structure.

'My Love for You', on the surface, seems to be a poem about a deeply loving relationship, where the speaker is delighting in explaining his love which is strong and true'. However, the poet uses line length to suggest there is a growing distance between the two people in the relationship. The rhyming couplets begin with eight syllables each:

My love for you is strong and true,
I could not survive without you,

However, the second line grows longer with each couplet. By the end, the second line is twelve syllables in length whereas the first line remains at eight syllables. Here, Chapman uses line length to symbolise the growing distance between the two lovers.

The speaker, perhaps represented by the first line, remains the same throughout. However, the second person, represented by line two, gets further and further away. The poet uses both structure and form to suggest an emotional distance between the speaker and listener in the poem.

This is reinforced with the final words of the poem 'my love will never die'. Although on the surface, the speaker is showing constancy with his love, these words might be implying that he knows her love for him is dying., i.e. *Even though your love is dying, my love will never die.* Perhaps this explains why the poet places the verb 'die' as the last word of the poem: the poem is really about the death of her love.

NOTE: Remember my point from earlier in this guide about presenting a well-structured argument? My answer here essentially uses two separate parts of the poem to make one point. As a result, the argument is both cohesive and persuasive.

Now that we've mastered the art of analysing unseen poetry, let's look at how to compare unseen poems.

Comparing the Second Unseen Poem with the First (Section C, Question 2)

In question 2, the comparison question is likely to be very simple, such as:

In both 'My Love for You' and 'Bully', the speakers describe strong emotions. What are the similarities and/or differences between the ways the poets present those emotions?

[8 marks]

The second unseen poem will always be named in the question first, so always begin your answer by writing about the second unseen poem. (This is the examiner's way of encouraging you not to repeat everything that you have already written for question 1.)

As you can see, this question is worth 8 marks, and will probably only require 10 -13 minutes of effort, which includes annotating and choosing which points to make. To achieve full marks in the question, you need to give an exploratory comparison with precise references. In other words, you need to compare with short, ideally single-word quotations.

A reminder that to hit top marks, you need to analyse the poets' use of language, form **and** structure.

Something important to notice here is that the question is not 'what are the strong emotions' but 'how are the strong emotions presented'. This means looking at the use of language, form and structure, analysing how they are used to convey meaning.

SAMPLE ANSWER:

Both poems appear to express an emotion but they use language, form and structure to hint at deeper feelings.

'Bully' seems to be explaining a problematic relationship, asking 'why do you always have to be so mean?'. However, the form of the poem is a near perfect sonnet—a form of love poetry, so the form seems to contradict the topic of the poem. In the volta, it is a shock to learn that the speaker has married the childhood bully. This makes the reader re-evaluate the title 'Bully', as there are hints that the speaker is being bullied in his marriage and is suffering domestic violence. Perhaps he is not so open about explaining his emotions as in society, it might be seen as unmanly for a man to be bullied by his wife.

Similarly, 'My Love for You' appears to express an emotion but it suggests something else. At first glance, it seems to be a lyric poem in which the speaker delights that his love is 'real and strong'. However, the poet uses line length to suggest there is a growing distance between the two people in the relationship. The odd-numbered lines of eight syllables represent the speaker and remain the same throughout, perhaps symbolising the constancy of the speaker's love. In contrast, the even-numbered lines, representing the listener, increase in syllables and finish at 12 syllables. This might symbolise the growing distance between the couple. This hints at underlying feelings of desperation and sadness because the speaker is aware that his love is not reciprocated. This is reinforced with the final words of the poem 'my love will never die'. Although on the surface, the speaker is expressing his love, he might be accusatory in tone with the stress on 'my love' as opposed to hers. Perhaps this explains why the poet places the verb 'die' as the last word of the poem: the poem is really about the death of her love.

As you can see, I only really had time to explain one point in full detail. It's better to write a lot about a little than to make five different points very briefly.

An introduction and conclusion are not necessary, as you are not asked to write an essay and you won't have time to include them. However, a single sentence to explain your thread of discussion would add cohesion to your response.

Finally, I'd like to wish you the best of luck in your exams. Check out my YouTube channel at https://www.youtube.com/user/mrbruff/playlists. If you've written a particularly good literature essay, email it to me info@mrbruff.com and I might use it in my next YouTube video!

Printed in Great Britain
by Amazon